LADIES OF THE NIGHT

LADIES OF THE NIGHT

by
SUSAN HALL

with photographs by
BOB ADELMAN

A Prairie House Book

Published by Trident Press
A Division of Simon & Schuster, Inc.
Rockefeller Center
630 Fifth Avenue
New York, New York 10020

FIRST PRINTING

SBN: 27114

LIBRARY OF CONGRESS
CATALOG CARD NUMBER: 73-11738

DESIGNED BY DON DUFFY

Manufactured in the
United States of America

AUTHORS' NOTE

WHORES ARE OUTCASTS. Criminals. Rejects completely accepted only by pimps. They offend our moral sense. Their work converts the most intimate act between men and women into commerce. Unfortunately, customers are not practicing moralists—except perhaps later. For lonely men and travelers, for business men making deals, for men with sexual hang-ups and men who want hassle-free sex, whores are a seeming necessity. In exchange for their services, prostitutes are paid, sometimes jailed, and socially stigmatized.

The act of prostitution is relatively innocuous. It involves two consenting adults in an exchange of money for services. There may or may not be satisfaction, but neither party appears to be wronged. Still, throughout most of the United States, we label prostitution a crime, make the women criminals, and repress their activities.

Laws that impose the morality of some on others are undesirable and experience suggests that laws that go against the needs and practices of a large number of people are unenforceable. Witness the history of gambling and prohibition legislation.

Real crimes are connected with prostitution, however. These are associated with the chaos of street life. A street girl protected by anonymity will probably swipe a wallet if she's given a chance, but a madam building a clientele is likely to return a lost wallet untouched.

In most English speaking nations (and in the United Nations recommendation), a prostitute has the right to choose her work. Only street solicitation is curbed. The virtue of this policy is to allow the prostitute to work without bothering the rest of us, and to minimize the amount of time the police must devote to prostitution. For instance, in the center of New York City, as much as half of the police force's time and effort is devoted to enforcing anti-prostitution laws, while drug epidemics and major crimes mushroom.

Society finds prostitution degrading. Since prostitution is both criminal and condemned, it is difficult to gauge how satisfying the work is. The girls internalize our condemnation and often hate what they do. Speculatively, if prostitution were decriminalized, would the work take on a different meaning? A few girls in the book viewed themselves as sex therapists and social workers. From the prostitutes' point of view, a low-paying, hum-drum office job is more degrading. The act of prostitution is what it is. Our policies and views make a crime out of what could possibly be useful work.

LADIES OF THE NIGHT grew out of extensive conversations with prostitutes and candid observations of their lives. The subjects we have selected are representative of crucial aspects of "the life." Most of the conversations were held in the girls' working environments—the street, massage parlors, hotels, apartments and madams' houses. While we have chosen to structure the book in a hierarchy from the street girl to the high class girl, a prostitute's work is, in fact, fluid. In one day, a girl might work the street, a massage parlor and from a phone in her own apartment. An ambitious girl works where there is work. We have tried, in both the photographs and text, to establish the girls as they live and to present them as they see themselves. The text is in the girls' own language, but shaped by our preoccupation with the costs and satisfactions of their way of life.

In LADIES OF THE NIGHT, you will come to know some prostitutes. We hope to ease your estrangement from these women. What follows is life among the condemned.

—SUSAN HALL AND BOB ADELMAN

ACKNOWLEDGEMENTS

I wish to thank all the "ladies" who gave so generously of their time and themselves. I hope that this book reflects their feelings and attitudes.

Several other ladies have read and re-read the manuscript as it developed: Joyce Johnson, Harriet McDougal, and particularly my friend Elaine Edelman have made invaluable contributions. Grace Shaw has supported me through two difficult projects, and this book has been formed with her encouragement and direction.

Bob Adelman photographed these "ladies," but he has also applied his acute critical judgment to the text. I want to thank him for his collaboration. —Susan Hall

CONTENTS

ON THE STREET

KITTY

ON THE STREET

KITTY
a Down 'Ho

KITTY: In New York, there are three different big strolls—places where prostitutes go to work. West Side girls around Times Square and Eighth Avenue—they're mostly ten and twenty-dollar girls. That's the price of a trick you find on Broadway. Cheap! If you're lucky, you might catch twenty Johns a night and make some decent money.

Fifty-seventh near Riker's, and Lexington around 49th—here you meet the more expensive trick. The girls have a bit more class. We give a guy more than head. Instead of going to a dirty bed in a hotel, they come to our apartments.

I've worked the stroll in Washington [D.C.], and there's not as much business as New York. The cops are after you every minute What's more, you automatically do time if they catch you in the capital. In New York, you can get charged with disorderly conduct and walk the next day. You just go to court and pay.

I feel safe in a town with a stroll. If I'm broke, I can always go out and earn my food and rent. Once I went to Las Vegas. I didn't have any contacts, but I figured the first girl who'd gone out there didn't have a connection! Well, I got to town and couldn't make contact. In almost any other city I know, I could have walked the street. But in Vegas, there's just one street and that ain't no street at all. There's no dates and plenty of cops. I panicked and came back to New York right away.

I've always thought of myself as a street girl. Street girls are down 'hos*—they don't know nothing but how to whore. And after a while, they don't want nothing else. No one has the right to say I should be a beautician. I don't want to curl people's funky hair!

I'm selling myself and I feel I should have a say-so over my own body. Besides, I could never go to work at eight and stay till five. Whenever I want, I go out on the street. You might think that typing is easier than fucking and better for you. But I don't know how to type.

Personally, I could live on nothing. But I have to talk to
* *Whores.*

other girls on the stroll. If my friend Sandy says, "I got a mink jacket for Christmas," I want to be able to say, "I got a mink coat." I want to look good, even though I don't have to. The "life" means something to me. I love my pimp and I want to make him look good too.

I couldn't do nothing at all, because I have to have money. I couldn't be kept. If I were kept by my pimp, Daddy, I just wouldn't be happy. I like to give him money. It's giving him of myself, because the money comes from my body. I'm giving more of myself by turning a trick for fifty dollars than I possibly could by just laying up with him.

Prostitution may be degrading. I'm putting myself down. But I feel good when *I* think a man thinks enough of me to pay for me. Anyway, I'm doing this for Daddy. And Daddy's never happier than when he's just got something for himself with my money. After he buys six new pairs of boots, he's just like a little boy.

Pimping is illegal too. It should definitely be legalized. Daddy may be selling me, but it is *my choice*. He does not force me to do nothing. I'm on the street for him, because I want to be.

KITTY: I've been working on the street for four years. Lexington and 49th is my corner. It's the only place I've ever worked. I know everyone in the whole area—every hotel owner, house detective, bellman, and elevator man. I know every cop on the street.

Usually I stand in front of the old Shelton Towers or the Belmont

Plaza. I'm standing right next to the hotel man and he'll say, "How's business going?"

I say, "Terrible," and go into the hotel to make a phone call. After a while you learn people's names. I know the coffee-shop attendants. They don't look down on me, 'cause prostitutes give bigger tips.

I always buy Ultima II products in the drugstore. When I go to the counter, the man says, "Ultima II what today, Kitty?" When I go up front, the guy pulls out a package of Dentine gum and Kools. That's what I always get. We'll be talking and he'll say, "I hear a couple of girls got arrested. Be careful." Even if he didn't hear that, he'll say it to start a conversation. He'll say, "You look nice tonight." Little things like that.

If I'm having an argument with a trick in front of the drugstore and he's calling me a dirty whore, the drugstore man will come out and say, "Leave this girl alone. She happens to be my girlfriend. If you do anything to her, I'll break your head open." My friends don't go too much out of their way to protect me, but if they see someone bothering me, they'd stop him.

I've been on this corner longer than any other girl. I'm jealous when a new girl comes out to work. Last night I see two little girls I've never seen before whispering on my corner. They're talking about me: "I wish these girls would stop coming over from the West Side." They think *I'm* new.

I go over to them: "Who are you referring to?"

"You. You weren't out here last night."

"Maybe last night I wasn't out here, but I've been out here for four years. You go back to the West Side where you came from." They leave, but I'm really mad.

Last week, there's a new cop on the beat. He says, "Get off my beat!"

I say, "No. You get off *my* beat."

The cop says, "I've been here for eight months."

"But I've been here for four years. This is my corner. If you don't think both of us can make it together, I suggest you find another beat." He laughs. He's too young to make trouble. Doesn't know how.

Every guy knows he can find a girl on 49th and Lexington in New York. Maybe a guy comes back because the first girl he ever went with was on 49th. Like I bought my first pocketbook at I. Miller's and I liked it. I always go back to I. Miller's for pocketbooks. I might not like an individual pocketbook that well, but I like I. Miller's. These guys like Lexington and 49th. I tell my regulars, "You can call me and, if I'm not home, I'll be on 49th."

If I go out with three or four guys a night, two or three of them I've seen before. They find me standing by the lamplight. Sometimes I wear my hair different and they don't recognize me. They say, "Do you know Kitty?"

I say, "Yeah, but she's out of town. Do you want to go with me?"

"No. I like Kitty."

I start to tease. "Why don't you come with me? Is Kitty cuter?"

"Yeah."

"Is she nicer than me?"

"Yeah, she's nicer than you. There's nobody like Kitty."

I say, "Well, I am Kitty."

"How can you prove it?"

"Come home with me. I'll show you the tattoos on my titties." That's the way I prove I'm Kitty.

Sometimes me and my man * Daddy drive up Park Avenue in his car. Everyone looks. They think: "That poor bitch must sell a lot of pussy." But it makes me real proud, because I bought that Eldorado for him and he's happy with it. I'm madly in love with Daddy. I don't know which is worse. Spending the rest of my life with him or without him. If I left, I'd be miserable all the time. If I'm with him, I'm miserable some of the time.

There's just something about Daddy. He understands all women. I definitely find him sexually attractive. I've been with straight guys. I haven't been a whore all my life. A straight guy thinks you're cheating on him when you're working. I asked one guy: "Why are you going out with all these girls? I don't fool around. When I want to see you, I can't, because you're busy." I fuck for business and he was

* _Pimp._

fucking for fun. Straight guys don't understand. They never will.

Daddy and me pass Park and 49th and I look over to Lexington. He says, "Can't stand it? Can't stand being away from home, can you?" I know every crack in the sidewalk. I know every brick in the walls. I know every nook and cranny where I can go hide from the cops. I can run to the drugstore and they'll put me behind the counter. The cops come in and search the place, think I must have run out the other door and go onto the street again. I'm safe on Lexington and 49th. It's home.

I grew up in the Midwest. Everything I used to do, my mother didn't care. She didn't say anything. She brought me up because she didn't know no better.

My favorite girlfriend's mother always beat her up for every little thing she did. I tried to talk her into running away from home when we were twelve. Her mother beat her. She said, "The only reason I do this is because I love you and I don't want you doing bad things."

I started thinking my mother didn't love me. She never hollered at me and I *was* a bad girl. I started disrespecting her. Everything she asked me to do, I wouldn't do on purpose. On school days I was supposed to be home by six o'clock. I wouldn't come home. She didn't even holler when I didn't go to school at all.

Then I started doing really bad things—stealing cars. She'd say, "Kitty. Why did you do that? Do you want me to buy you a new dress? Or a new pair of shoes?"

Now my mother was really prejudiced and I thought I might get her angry if I hung around with colored people. I found an ugly black guy and brought him home. She got really angry. But just then I was caught stealing cars and sent away.

One day in jail they came and told me my mother was getting divorced. My father had said he'd kill her if she ever left him. Then I was listening on the radio and heard that a man had shot his wife and hisself. They didn't say it was my parents, but I knew. The prison people called me in and just looked at me.

When I got out of jail, I came to New York to get a job. I was

sixteen. I walked right into Mickey Walker's bar on 49th and Eighth.
I looked out of place, so the bouncer came up and says, "Can I help
you? Do you know where you are?"

"I had an appointment for a job. I was supposed to speak to the
manager." He told me to wait.

I sat down in a booth and this girl came over and told me a friend
of hers was at the bar and would like to have a drink. I thought this
was a good play, because the manager would think I could get along
with people. I don't drink, but I ordered Chivas Regal, because I
knew it was an expensive Scotch.

I'm sitting at the bar when the manager comes over and gives me
the job: "Don't tell me how old you are. You're over eighteen.
At least twenty-one. Right?"

"Right."

He tells me to be back for work that night. The girl is still sitting
by me and asks whether I've ever partied before. Now partying to
me isn't two girls and a guy—partying is going out dancing. I said,
"Yeah. What do you think I am, a square?" A square means a person who doesn't swing.

She looks at me like she thinks I'm square, but I'm going to prove
I'm not. We get in a guy's car and he drives us to Queens. Today I
wouldn't go all the way to Queens with a trick. Not unless he had
a special high price.

We go to this guy's house and he asks if I want a drink. I didn't
want him to think I was stupid, so I said yeah. I'm sitting there sip-
ping my drink and there's no people coming. I turn to him:
"Where's all the people?" She takes off her clothes. So does he. I
don't know where I'm at. We drove a long way. Here's a man and
a girl. I think they're friends and they want to rape me. So I says to
myself, I'm not a virgin. I may as well let them fuck me, instead of
having them fight me and beat me up or kill me. So I take off all my
clothes and the guy wants to see the girl go down on me. You're not
supposed to with a trick. You just pretend—get close and put your
arms around. But she really did it to me.

The girl left and I saw the man give her some money. Even then

I had a little bit of game * and a bit of sense. While he was driving me back to the city, I started crying. He asks why. I said he'd given her money, but he didn't give me none. By then I knew she was a prostitute. He tells me I'm an innocent kid and he feels kind of bad. He thought I was a working girl. He gives me twenty dollars. And I start crying again. He says, "Why are you still crying?"

"Because I need forty dollars for my rent. I just came to New York and if I don't pay my rent, I don't have no place to go." So he gives me twenty dollars more. Then he gives me ten more.

He says, "Now you have some money. Try not to do this no more." He's being really nice.

I goes to my friend's house and shows her the money: "Look. Fifty dollars." I told her the boss had advanced me pay.

"They don't do things like that. I know how you got this money." She was real mad. She took the money and tore it up. She told me if I ever needed money to ask her for it and never to do what I did again. I said okay.

I started working in the bar and knowing pimps and prostitutes. The pimps wore lemon and lime and raspberry suits—the Kool-Ade colors. I thought they were movie stars.

One girl keeps coming to the bar every night and bothering me to visit her. I was so lonesome that I rang her buzzer one night. This guy answers and says, "Jennie's not home, but come on up. She's expecting you. She should be home shortly."

I go up and this guy starts talking: "I'm Jennie's boyfriend and her business manager." I didn't know this added up to pimp. He gives me some wine to drink. I'm getting high by the contact of his reefer coming at me. Jennie doesn't come home. Finally he tells me she's called. "Jennie's coming home, but she'll be late."

I'm so tired from drinking wine I don't want to go home. Everything seems so nice. He says I can rest in the bedroom till Jennie comes. A couple of hours later, he walks in: "Will you do me a favor? There's a guy here. He wants to see you and he'll give you fifty dollars. You don't have to have sex. Just tell him dirty stories."

This keeps happening—guys coming in every once in a while.

* *A whore's strategy in working the street.*

Finally I had sex with one man. By that time I had three hundred dollars. I'd never seen that in one pile.

Jennie comes home and says how much she appreciates me seeing all those guys. I says, "Guess what? I made three hundred dollars. I've never had three hundred dollars in my life."

So she says, "Maybe you should give some of it to him. Just go talk to him. Maybe he could hold your money."

So I went to the bedroom and says to him, "You know I made three hundred dollars." I gives him twenty. He didn't do nothing. I did it. He couldn't have made that money unless I was there.

I tells Jennie, "I gave him some money."

"How much did you give him?"

"I gave him twenty dollars."

"And you made three hundred? Every day you can make this money. You should make him your manager and your boyfriend."

So I gives him the three hundred dollars, which was all his to begin with, because he'd give fifty bucks to a guy and say, "I want you to give it to the bitch. She'll give it back to me anyhow."

Once they knew I'd turn tricks for real, I started taking dates off the phone—twenty-, thirty-, and forty-dollar tricks. And then they put me out on the street.

Now I know all the girls on the stroll.* Girls come and go. Some move to the West Side. Others leave town. I lose touch with them, even though I stay.

I usually get out around eleven o'clock. I'll see a girlfriend and say, "Hi," and walk on down the stroll. I won't block her action. Especially if it's a colored girl. If a guy sees her first, he'll say, "Want to go out?" But if I'm there, he'll come straight for me—because I'm white.

I might start talking to a new girl: "Seen any cops around? How long have you been out here?"

"About an hour. I don't think the cops are out yet."

"Have you been picking up?"

"I broke luck.** Made fifty dollars." That's all we might say to

* Locale where prostitutes work and walk.
** Caught her first trick, i.e. John.

each other. The next night, I see her again, and she says, "How're you doing?"

I say, "Okay." We don't know each other's names. We might never know each other's names. But we'll be chatting and all of a sudden I'll say, "Who are you with?"

She says, "Fast Red. Who're you with?"

"Daddy."

"You're with Daddy? I know Suzy [a wife-in-law *]. What's your name?"

"Kitty."

"Yes. I've heard of you."

Maybe next week she isn't out. I'll ask someone, "What happened to that cute little white girl who used to be out here—the one with the blond hair who always wore a blue coat?"

"Mary?"

"I never knew her name."

"Yeah. That must be Mary. She's on the West Side now."

Almost nobody calls each other by their name. We say, "Girlfriend." Maybe I catch a date and you're standing across the street. I know your name is Sharon and I think I've heard you using Paula for tricks. But I'm not sure. I'll shout, "Hey, girlfriend." You come over and I introduce you as a friend of mine. I ask the guy if he wants to go with both of us. I'll say, "This is John." Right away you say, "My name is Paula." Girls use different names for jail, for tricks, for their own man, and for the street. I'm unusual. I just use Kitty.

There are different levels of prostitutes on the street. There are girls who are really dedicated and work. There are "jive bitches"—girls who just fool around. They talk all the time. I talk, but I still try to make my money. I bullshit enough to keep everybody happy that they're my friend, but I don't bullshit so much that I don't have time to catch a trick. If I'm talking and a trick comes along, I just turn around and say, "Hi, honey. You want to go out?" He'll keep walking on and I'll continue our conversation. Some girls wouldn't even stop talking. They don't try to catch tricks.

If I kept talking, all the girls would say, "I don't know how Daddy

_____
* *The relationship of one pimp's woman to another of his women.*

can have Kitty. She's always sitting around the coffee shop and bull-shitting on the corner. She never does any work. Probably makes fifty dollars a day, if she makes that much. Why doesn't her man kick her out?" They go home and be talking to their fellows and say, "You know Kitty? She's with Daddy. Man, I don't know how he can keep that bitch. She don't ever work." I'd get labeled.

Most of the girls on the street I like. We have a lot in common. We're prostitutes and we all have pimps. Some girls go to work, don't make no money, and are scared to go home, so they come over to my house after work. I'll cook them breakfast and then we talk: "A guy got me in a car last night and acted weird. I tried to talk my way out and had to fight." "I went with a guy and took four hundred dollars from him. He caught me and I didn't know how much money it was until he said four hundred. I fought to keep it." "Guess who's in jail?" "Guess who's back in town?" "Barbara chose Daddy." * "Do you know a girl named Linda? Well, check her out. She just chose my man." If you know her, you say, "She's real flaky and never stays with no guy. She doesn't make any money. She dresses dumb and she's stupid." That kind of stuff.

The girls sleep over at my house till one o'clock the next day. Then they mess up their hair, ruin their make-up, and tell their fellow they've been in jail.

Girls on the street are my friends as far as a friend on the street can go, but they'll cross you in a minute. Let's say we both go with one date and know we'll steal money from him. The guy lies down at the end of the bed and puts his clothes on the table. She'll be frenching him and I'll be sitting in front of him, leaning over and touching him so he can't see. She'll reach in his pocket, take the money, and stick it under her bed. Then she'll say, "Okay Kitty. You fuck." But like she might steal a hundred dollars and only give me thirty. You're supposed to split fifty-fifty.

Maybe I'll be rapping with a girl and say something about my man. She goes home and tells her fellow: "You know what Kitty said about Daddy?" That gets back to Daddy and I get in trouble.

* *Picked him as her pimp.*

The girl doesn't do it for any special reason. It's just to start shit. 'Hos just like to start shit. It keeps you going. It's exciting.

Girls respect me because I'm dedicated. I'm dedicated to my work and to my man. Some girls I won't even speak to, because, if I did, they'd be hanging on me all night. Prostitutes don't respect flaky girls. Like if someone said, "Who are you with?" I'd say, "Daddy."

The next day, she says, "How's Daddy?"

I say, "I don't know. I'm with Flash."

Next day, "Hi, Kitty. How's Flash?"

"Flash who? Oh, Flash. I left him three days ago. I'm with Charlie." Or Vinnie. Or Mr. C. You just don't have respect for a person like that. I'm not flaky. I don't run off from my fellow all the time.

I also have a fair reputation. Nobody would bother me. All the girls that are badder than me and could really hurt me, I make it my business that they're my friends. Maybe there's one girl on the street that can't stand me. But that girl's got to fight me and Mary and Ellen and Alice and everyone else. Anyway, we don't have time to fight. We have to catch a trick. If I'm fighting with a girl, I'm going to miss a trick and I'll be fighting with Daddy for making no money. I'll have two fights. I don't mind one.

All Daddy's women are supposed to stand together. If one gets in trouble, the others have to help. One of my wives-in-law, Sherry, a lot of girls were bothering her and saying they were going to take her mink coat. Shit like that. Sherry doesn't say nothing. She's always coming to me. I tell the girls to leave her alone. Whether I hate her or love her, I've got to protect her, because she's my man's business. If you hit Daddy, I'd try to kill you. Sherry's part of Daddy.

This one night, we all got put in jail. In the bull pen, one girl, Stephanie, called Daddy a punk. I couldn't fight in the bull pen. I had had three cheese sandwiches and was really sick. But as soon as we got out, Stephanie, she starts sticking her finger in Sherry's face and says, "If I ever catch you without Kitty, I'm going to give it to you." I tell Stephanie to leave the girl alone. I don't feel like fighting 'cause I'm sick.

The next night, Stephanie gets Sherry alone on the street. She hits her in the face. So Sherry comes up and says, "Kitty, she hit me."

I says, "Go hit her back. You can't let a girl hit you. If she thinks you're a punk, she's always going to bother you."

Sherry says, "She's going to kick my ass."

"So what? You go over to Stephanie and hit her in the face and then start fighting. If it looks like you're losing, I'll come over and whip her ass, because I've got to whip her anyway for calling Daddy a punk." I explain that I don't want it to look like I'm helping her.

"But Kitty. All the other girls will come and help her." All the girls think Sherry's a snob. As a matter of fact she is. She's prejudiced against prostitutes.

I says, "Those girls can't. They've got to be getting their money together. How can they go home and tell their fellows they don't have any money because they were beating up Daddy's woman?"

Sherry just caught a date and went off. But a little colored girl came up to me and said, "How's Sherry feel, Kitty?" That burnt me up. I didn't want to walk away from no fucking fight and that was an invitation to fight.

I went and smacked Stephanie in the mouth. "How do you feel, bitch?" We start fighting and she pulls a knife on me. I don't carry a knife, so I just kicked her purse. Everything flew out. My hair's all over my face and I'm trying to keep away from the bitch's knife. She's got her knife at my throat.

"Kitty. I know you don't want to die, but I'm going to cut your motherfucking throat."

All of a sudden, the cops comes by and grabs her and me and takes us to jail. I call Daddy. He's already heard about it, because everyone called him and told him what happened.

I says, "I'm in jail for fighting, but I'll be out in the morning."

He says, "Is she bleeding? I want to see blood."

Meanwhile, Stephanie keeps trying to talk to me. Me and her are very good friends and she knows I'm going to kick her ass. The bitch can fight with a knife, but she can't use her hands. She says, "It's over with?"

I says, "Yes. It's over with. Our friendship is over with. Finished."

"Why do you want to get into your wife-in-law's affairs?"

"It's my man's affairs. If you never did nothing to Sherry, I was going to get you anyway for calling my man a punk."

In the morning, she says, "Can we share a cab home?"

"Yeah." I didn't say one word to her in the cab. The bitch sets herself up. I'm just smiling.

She says, "Why aren't you talking to me? Are you still mad?"

"Yes. I'm still mad. I'm kicking your fucking ass as soon as I get out of the cab."

In front of Daddy's building, she tries to run from me, but I throw her into the lobby. I keep hitting her. She won't hit back. She won't defend herself.

I says, "You slapped me. You called my fellow a punk. Now you fight." She still won't fight.

The doorman tells me to leave her alone. "If you guys want to fight, take it outside."

Stephanie grabs hold of a pillar in the lobby. I try to drag her out. The doorman says, "Kitty, if you don't stop that, I'm going to call Daddy and tell him to come down."

"Call Daddy. I don't give a fuck."

Daddy comes down and laughs. The doorman says, "Make her stop, Daddy!"

Then I go really crazy, because the bitch won't fight. She won't do nothing. I feel like a big old fool, because she won't hit back. I'm even madder. I'm trying to kill her. Daddy says stop and I don't. The doorman says, "She's going to kill the girl."

Daddy says, "I can make her stop. I can make her do anything I want." So I stop and go to Daddy. We go up the stairway with Stephanie. I tell Daddy that Stephanie called him a punk. Then he lets me fight her until she bleeds. You've got to fight for your honor.

On the street, you don't try to steal each other's dates. You don't undercut another girl. Say I go for thirty dollars and I'm standing next to you and you go for fifty. A guy comes up to you and you say, "Fifty. I can't go for less than fifty. Okay? Is that all right?"

He says, "That's too much. I go for thirty." I'm standing right next to you, but I wouldn't take him. Even if I can't stand you, he asked you first and I'm not going to go second to nobody. No one wants to put themselves down in front of another girl. I'm not going to go for less than fifty, because I think I'm as good as you, if not better. If a guy is spending a hundred and you say two hundred, I wouldn't go for a hundred, because he might think I'm less than you. Sometimes I'll be talking to a guy and he'll say, "How much?"

"Fifty."

"The girl over there told me twenty," he says.

"Go with her!" I go for fifty and if some guys wants me and fifty is too much, the girl next to me might say, "Kitty, shit, I need the money."

I'll say, "Go with him." As long as she asks, it's okay.

We try to work in pairs, because you can make more money and it's easier. If I catch a trick, I'm going to try to get a friend of mine to come with us. Let's say another girl is standing next to me and you're across the street. I'll say to the trick, "My best friend's standing across the street. We'll go with her."

He says, "No, I want the girl standing next to you."

"If you don't go with the other girl who's my friend, you don't go with me." I'm going to take my best friend first. Why should I help someone I don't like?

If you and me were standing together and you catch a trick for fifty dollars, you'd say, "You want to party with two girls?"

He'd say, "What's a party?"

I'd say, "Two girls. Both of us at the same time." A guy won't spend fifty a piece. He might spend thirty or forty. But for ten or twenty dollars more, he gets another girl. The guy can still only go one time. One girl frenches and the other fucks. We're both cutting our money, but the guy is excited and comes quicker. You can also steal from him. If there's a fight, two girls can win. If your stomach hurts, or you've got your period, it's better to work with another girl. So you french and I fuck. Next week, I may have my period and I do the frenching. That's just if we're working together on a trick.

I do fuck when I have my period. When I come into the apartment, I wash off. I put something under me so the sheets don't get dirty. I quickly wipe his thing afterwards so he doesn't notice. He don't ever know.

I could never tell Daddy I didn't work because I had my period. He has sex with me then, just to make the point: "If you can have sex with me, you can go and turn a trick."

One time when I was really sick with the flu, I called Daddy and said, "I'm leaving you, 'cause I'm really, really sick."

"What are you leaving for?"

"I can't work. I'm sick and I don't want you to be mad at me."

"Don't be silly. If you're sick, stay home and go to bed. I'll be right over. What do you think I am, a slave driver?"

He came to my place and we did it. Sometimes when you're sickly, you can be with your man, but you just can't stand on the street.

Daddy started laughing afterwards. I says, "What's so funny?"

"I thought you were too sick. It takes more energy to go to bed with me than it does with a trick." So I had to go to work. It's all game. I have sex with Daddy when I'm sick. I have sex with him when I have my period. I don't have no excuses about work.

Actually, I worked until I was eight months pregnant. Guys believe that pregnant pussy is best. I could give the saddest little sympathy story and play on them.

If I wore a coat, it was hard to tell I was pregnant. I got the biggest kick with guys who were looking for a prostitute because their own wife was pregnant. A guy would come up and say, "You're really cute. What are you doing out on the street?"

I'd say, "What are *you* doing out on the street?"

"My wife is having a baby and you know you shouldn't do anything with pregnant women." We'd get up to the room and he'd say, "Oh, my God. You're pregnant too." I had a ball.

I cooked up a good story. I told men that I'd been in college and I went with a boy and wouldn't let him go to bed with me. Then I let him, got pregnant and he didn't want me no more. My parents kicked me out of the house and this was the only way I could take care of the baby. I had to make money. I was alone. With nobody.

Men respected me. "You're a brave little girl." They'd give me money and wouldn't even touch me. I'd say I couldn't fuck because it would hurt the baby. Frenching would make me sick to my stomach. Most decent guys didn't make me do anything. I'd jerk some off with my hand. They'd say, "Here's thirty for you and ten more for the baby." I made a lot of money when I was pregnant. And I didn't have to work as hard. The cops didn't chase me. They be scared I'd run and fall down and hurt myself. I got a lot of sympathy, and I didn't have no sex.

Usually I can't stand tricks. When you're turned out,* pimps put that in your head. "You don't get off with tricks." Tricks are tricks—that's how they got the name. When they turn around and satisfy you, you're the trick. And tricks ain't shit.

I could never walk down the street if I started digging a trick. I could never say to my girlfriend, "Guess who called? Paul. He used to be a trick of mine. Now he's my boyfriend."

She'd say, "What? Are you kidding me?"

Maybe I'd see Daddy and he'd say, "How are you and your fucking trick getting along?" I couldn't stand things people would say. It's something you don't do in the life. You don't go with tricks.

Some tricks can be useful. I got a trick who's in the carpet business. I can get a carpet for cheaper and fuck most of it off. I meet a guy and he says he's in the furniture business. I say, "Oh, really. I need furniture for my living room." Or he's a drapery man or a grocery man. I don't do too much bartering, because you give up cash, and if Daddy don't want me to have something, I can't have it.

It's sex with tricks that I hate. Sex is horrible. Just horrible. I used to be able to stand it, but now I close my eyes and keep thinking it's a dog fucking me. It's just disgusting. If I didn't have a strong mind, I would go off—crazy. I guess with girls sex is emotional and with men it's physical. A man can put it in a coke bottle and push in and out and come.

My guys have to have pretty straight tastes. If they want something stupid, I won't do it. Anything other than fucking is stupid. I'll suck

* *Become a prostitute.*

them and they can get on me. If a guy says, "Get on top of me," I say no. If I'm on top, he might be getting ready to come, I might stop and then have to start all over again. I won't let men touch me. I won't let them suck my titties. Hell, no.

I get on the bottom and I don't have nothing to do. They do all the work. I've got a trick who comes to me every week. He says, "How do you feel? Are you in a good mood?" If I say I'm tired or I've got a cold, he'll just give me thirty dollars and sit rapping with me for a few minutes and go. If he thinks I can't enjoy it, he won't do anything with me.

He says, "You like it?"

"Of course I like it. I wouldn't do it unless I did." You can make a guy believe anything.

He says, "But you do it for money."

"Money doesn't mean anything for me. If I could dig typing letters, I'd be a secretary. I just dig sex."

Last night a friend brought a guy to me. His wife died a year ago and he hadn't been to bed with a girl for a whole year. So I go down on him and he says, "Kitty. You don't have to do that. I just want you to love me. Just love me. You don't have to make me hard."

I said, "I just want to make you feel good and suck your dick. That's what makes me happy, because it makes you happy. Just lay back and relax." In two seconds he came, by thinking I really enjoyed making him happy.

Usually when I get a guy up to the apartment, I get the money and then I light a cigarette and put it in the ashtray. When the cigarette burns out, I know the time is up.

Some men can't get hard by your frenching them or nothing. They just want to sit there and hold you in their arms. You have to act like you like them and shit. They're hungry for affection.

A lot of men just don't come. If you stayed with them long enough, they might. But three minutes isn't long enough. If a man is nice about it, I say, "What's wrong with you? How come you can't come?" If he says, "I'm ready. I can come in a few seconds," I'll give him a few more seconds. Maybe a minute. That's the most I can give.

Or sometimes I say, "You must have been drinking, otherwise you're not much of a man." I know they haven't been drinking, but they say they've had five martinis. I say, "That must have did it." That gives them an excuse.

I might say, "Maybe you need a raincheck?" They think a raincheck means coming back and seeing me for nothing. But when I see them on the street and they say, "Remember me? I got a raincheck," I say, "Yeah, and so did fifty other people who spent money twice." They spend money again.

I see about five guys a night—the price depends. One might spend seventy-five, two might spend twenty-five, and another forty. You don't always fuck. Sometimes you just french. But that makes your teeth rotten. If it drips and gets in your gums, your mouth rots. My doctor told me that. I'm just getting to be one unhealthy bitch. I'm in the doctor's office every week with something—an irritated womb, a swollen vagina. What ruins me is having sex with Daddy after I have sex with tricks. I hurt. He's really big and good. Then I go to work and have it with five or six guys and get irritated.

Sometimes I go over to Daddy's house after work and say, "You know, I must have fucked a hundred guys. What do you think about that? How does that make you feel?"

He says, "How much did they spend?" Shit like that he says.

I says, "Don't you think any less of me? I mean, when you call up and I say I'm busy and you know I'm having sex with a guy and you say, 'As soon as you're finished, come over here,' and when I come over, I've just had sex with another guy?"

He says, "You know I like you and I don't think about you and other guys. I try not to think about it. When I do, I'm a little sad. But you're lucky to have heart enough to turn tricks or you couldn't have me."

Mine and Daddy's relationship—that's the only thing we have: sex. That's the major part of our relationship. I have never come with Daddy. I'm trying so hard to please him, I can't come. That worries me. Sometimes I think I should go to a psychiatrist. I need help.

Daddy is important to me, because I have to prove I can have a healthy sexual relationship. It's particularly important for a prostitute—after you've been with the animals. I never come with tricks. One time I wondered if I could. I said to myself, "Let's see if this motherfucker can make me come." I closed my eyes and pretended it was Daddy. I came. I found out I can come with a trick if I think about Daddy. I don't make a habit out of it, though. I tried one time to see if it worked, but that's cheating on Daddy.

I put myself down as a woman. I used to have confidence in myself. Guys liked *me*. Now the only thing I have is sex. I want to be fun to be with. Daddy takes his other girls out. But when he's in a groovy mood, he'll call me and we have sex.

Anything he wants to do, I do. I have anal sex with him. The first time, he said, "You're not going to believe this, but I've never done that before."

I said, "Do you think I have?"

About two months later, we did it again. Daddy has a terrible memory. He knows he's done something, but he can't remember which of his wife-in-laws he did it with.

After we did it, Daddy said, "That was the second time I've ever done that."

I said, "When was the first time?"

"A couple of months ago."

"Well, why didn't you do it with me first?"

"You should be glad I do it with you at all."

I says, "Well, this is the second time I did it."

"Who'd you do it with before?"

"You don't know?"

"Who?"

"Daddy!"

Daddy's always trying to show off when other people are around. I'll be sitting on the couch while he's goofing off with some guys and if my glance just happens to go to his pants, he'll say, "Ah, go on, take them down. Don't be shy because Roger's here. You're not shy!"

I'll say, "Oh, Daddy! Don't shout in front of Roger. Don't yell."

One time after he took a shower, I was drying him. I was on my knees—face to face with his cock. He's always saying, "Go on and bite on the big fellow." I thought I'd call his bluff. Roger was standing in the bathroom door, but I had all my clothes on. Daddy says, "Go on and bite the big fellow." I just grabbed it and put it in my mouth. I was all choked up with it.

He said, "Bitch. What's wrong with you? Roger's standing there." He pushed me away.

I said, "I'm just doing what you wanted me to."

"Man, get out of here. Get out of the bathroom door, Roger." Then he says to me, "How come you got so much heart all of a sudden? You won't suck it in the movies."

"What do you mean, Daddy? What was the name of the movie?"

He tries to think. Then he says, "It was Jean." That's really upsetting. He's not sure of what he does to who.

But I love Daddy very much. He never hits me for no reason. He hits me when I'm wrong. If he hit me for no reason whatsoever, then I would leave him. You have to do a lot of things wrong to make him mad. He lets things pile up. Even then, if you're having a good time together, he may just leave well enough alone. He won't mention anything. I know he knows and he's not going to let me know. Just to save the confusion of having a fight. Just to leave me be happy.

If he was cold-blooded, he wouldn't be Daddy. He walks around saying, "I'm too sweet. That's what's wrong with me." Sometimes he says, "You're going to turn me into a dirty old pimp again."

My head is with a pimp. If I wasn't with Daddy, I'd be with another pimp or a hustler—someone who would accept me as a prostitute. Maybe once in a while Daddy stops and thinks about all the men I go to bed with in one night. But it doesn't ruin our relationship. It makes it better. The more guys I see, the more money I get for Daddy. He knows I don't like seeing tricks. I'm doing it for him. If I had my mind on a white picket fence and a salesman for a husband, then the life would bother me. But I can't see myself with a guy like that. I can only be happy with a pimp. I need my own man.

I feel very dependent on Daddy. I feel helpless. I'm scared I might be so totally dependent on him I won't be able to do things for myself. What do I have? With Daddy, materially, I have an apartment and the clothes I wear. But I'm paying for this myself. He keeps telling me, "Bitch, if you leave me, you won't be nothing. You'll be a bum. How could you make it on your own?"

I say to myself, "Daddy, the money I give you is what's making these things possible for me. For every dress you buy me, you get five five-hundred-dollar suits." He puts it in my head that I can't make it without him. I'm really believing him.

When I leave Daddy, I might have four hundred dollars. I check into a hotel. Less the money I pay for the hotel, I buy a few things and, when my money runs out, I call Daddy. I'm basically lazy. I have to have a pimp to make money. If I'm by myself, I make just enough to get by. I don't have nothing. If I go to jail, I wouldn't get out. If something happens where I get sick for a couple of weeks and my rent's due, I can't pay it. With Daddy, I have security—financial security. He takes care of those expenses. I can't save money on my own, because I know I can make it again tomorrow. This is the way Daddy makes me think.

Of course, I do try to leave him. A few weeks ago, I went to a hotel room and then I called everybody I knew, because I wanted to go shopping. Nobody was at home, so I went out and bought two pairs of shoes and three pairs of boots. I spent almost three hundred dollars. I came home and wanted to tell someone what I bought. I called all my friends again. No one was home. So I called Daddy.

I said, "Hi. Are you sleeping? I'll call back when you wake up."

He said, "No. I think we'd better talk now."

"Go back to sleep. It's not important."

"What is it," he said.

"I just wanted to ask you a favor."

"What's that?"

"Can I go out and work tonight?"

"Sure."

"I'm not talking about going to work for you. I mean, is it safe for me to come out, because I don't have no money and I want to work the stroll."

"You can go work, but you have to come here first."

"I'm not going to."

"We've got to talk, Kitty."

"No, we don't. I know you, Daddy. You're just going to tell me all kinds of shit—anything—and then, when I'm back, you're going to do the same old shit all over again."

He said, "You're a dumb bitch. Can't you distinguish between what's game and what's real. Do I have to play on you?"

"Yes. If you treated me absolutely like you have been, I would leave. And if you treated me really, really nice, I would be with you and give you my money. So you have to be nice to me. Whether you like me or not, you have to act like you like me."

"Don't you know I like you?"

"Oh Daddy. Don't be silly."

"If I didn't like you, I'd kill you."

"You don't know where I'm at."

"Yes, I do."

"Where am I?"

"I'm not telling."

Finally Daddy convinced me to come see him. But I'm going to play on him and get him to take me out for the evening. I say, "You know, Daddy, I can't stand it without you, but I'm not going to stand for no more of your shit."

"All right," he says. "Come on over and talk."

"I'll get over sometime."

"Why can't you say you'll be over in a half an hour or an hour?"

"Because I'm not with you and I don't have to say that."

Daddy keeps saying, "Come on. Come on." I won't go.

So I says, "Why don't you come over here?"

"Where are you at?"

"I thought you knew."

"I don't know what room you're in." He didn't know which hotel I was in, but he was trying to make me tell him. I wasn't going to.

Finally I says, "Either I'm going to come down there and you're going to beat the hell out of me so I'll say, 'I got my ass kicked in and I may as well stay.' Or else you're going to be sweet and I'm going to think to myself, 'God, how can I leave him?' Either way, you've got me."

I go down to his apartment. First thing he says when I walk in the door is, "They're new shoes, aren't they?"

I says, "No."

He looks at them and says, "Are they?"

"You like them?"

"How much did they cost?"

"Thirty dollars."

"Thirty dollars for sandals! Didn't you ever hear of five-dollar sandals at bargain stores?"

"Did you?" We start laughing and he says, "They're kind of cute." Then he says we're going to see a show, but I don't want to see no show. I want to talk. So he takes me to the Wagon Wheel and makes me drink and drink. I don't drink nothing usually, so I'm getting ready to pass out. We go to a show and it's closed. So we go to a restaurant, but we can't go in, because Daddy refuses to take his hat off. His hair isn't done. We finally go back to his place.

Now a girl who's dancing at the Wagon Wheel calls Daddy and says she's coming over. So he tells me to start curling his hair. Then I have to give him a bath and lotion him down—get him ready for this stupid bitch. We don't say nothing.

Finally he turns around and says, "What time is it?"

"Quarter to four. The bar closes at four, so you'd better hurry up and get out of the tub."

He says, "We do have a little problem, don't we?"

I say, "Yeah," and go. That's the end of our discussion.

Daddy knows when one of his women is running off. I'm his woman and he knows me. He knows when he's done wrong. For two weeks, he'd promised to take me out. Then he got to threatening me. He wanted me to work in the daytime. I didn't want to. We were constantly fighting. But just over the phone. He knew I was leaving. If he'd jumped on me and beaten me up, I might have stayed, because we would have had it out. Instead, I had to leave to get the problems out in the open. Of course, we didn't get them straightened out, because Daddy never talks. He knows there's something wrong, but he tries to hide it.

Once I didn't see him for five days. He came over to my house, I cooked dinner and then he left. So I called and said, "I'm going to be a woman about the whole thing. You can have your fucking ring back. You can have your apartment and everything you bought me—which is nothing. You can even have the money I have now. I don't want your money. But I'll keep a hundred dollars, because I came with money." *

He says, "I'm on my way over."

"Are you going to beat me up?"

"What if I do and what if I don't?"

"Okay. I'm not scared. I'm scared, but I'm just going to be a woman about this."

He comes over and says, "Get dressed. You hear what I said? Get dressed. But first give me my money. All of it." So I give him all my money. Then he says, "I've got a cab waiting downstairs."

He takes me to another wife-in-law's for dinner. Some of my friends are there. But I won't talk to nobody. They say, "How're you doing Kitty?" I just grunt. They say, "What's wrong with you?" I don't say nothing.

Daddy calls me into the garden and says, "You know what you're going to do? Go over there and stand in the corner. Then I'm bringing everyone out here to laugh at you."

"Daddy. I'm not going to stand in the corner."

"Bitch, did you hear what I said?"

"I refuse, Daddy. I'd rather have you jump on me than stand in the corner in front of all these people." So I start laughing.

He says, "That's all I wanted to do. Make you laugh. Get out there and keep laughing. I don't care how hard it is, but you keep laughing. And whenever someone asks you something, you answer them

* *Brought him money like a dowry when she chose him.*

37

and add a bit to it." I'm real polite. And do what Daddy says.

Afterwards, we go over to his house, and, instead of asking me what's wrong, I have to tell him, "Daddy, I think you treat me worse than everybody." He does. And he admits it. I can do the same thing Sherry does and he'll beat me up and take Sherry out. Last time he jumped on me, he knocked me out. Out. Cold out.

After Daddy gets through beating you, he tells you to do a good make-up job and put on a wig, cover up your eyes and go to work. I've gone out on the stroll with two black eyes and nobody knew.

I do anything Daddy wants me to, because, when he's happy, everyone else in automatically happy. Not by anything he does. Just by his being happy. He loves to joke. I brought him pork chops one day. I didn't bring no bread, because he was on a diet. He had another girl in the apartment and said, "How do you expect me to eat this without bread?"

I said, "People manage to eat pork chops without bread. I think I can too."

"I want bread," says Daddy. "And when I want bread, I get bread. You go down to the restaurant and get me two slices of bread."

"Oh Daddy. I'm going to be embarrassed to get two slices of bread."

"Did you hear what I said?" He's showing off in front of his girl.

"I have a friend downstairs. I'll borrow two pieces."

"That's not what I told you to do. I told you to go to the restaurant and get two slices of bread. And get a receipt."

"I'm going to be embarrassed."

"You understand?" He's ordering.

I went to the restaurant and said, "I'm so embarrassed, but don't laugh and don't ask me why. Give me two slices of bread and I've got to have a receipt."

I came back and Daddy says, "Give me the receipt."

"I don't have one."

"Why not? Didn't I tell you to get one?"

The girl says, "What's going to happen?" She's really curious.

Daddy says, "Nothing, because Kitty has a receipt. That's what I told her to do. I'll put any amount of money on it."

The girl didn't think I had one. She thought Daddy was kidding. Then I gave Daddy the receipt. The girl said, "Why did she do that?"

"Because that's what I wanted her to do," says Daddy.

It was a fun thing. The girl was there wondering, "Is she or isn't she going to come back with the receipt?" I didn't want to get it, but I felt like I wanted to for Daddy.

I'm fighting Daddy a little now. He's trying to change my whole personality into Daddy. Talk to one of his other girls, and you can tell she's with Daddy. Her whole style is Daddy—the way she talks, the way she moves. When Daddy can tell a girl is going to stay, he works on her. He makes her him. I'm the only oddball. I just don't want to be a robot. I don't want to be Daddy. I want to be Kitty.

This is the problem. Daddy is the best pimp around. I have to have a pimp and I've looked at them all. I couldn't ever get adjusted to another life. This life is graduated. I feel I'm higher than other people. I'm better. I broke all the rules. I don't care if I go to jail. I just don't go along with what's supposed to be. You're not supposed to be a prostitute. You're not supposed to sell your body. But being a prostitute makes me enough money to do what I want to do—be in this life. Even though I give my money away, I give it by my own free choice. I make more money than most girls and I don't have to go out and work. The average, ordinary girl—a little secretary—has to be at work at nine in the morning till five. If she doesn't get her work done, she gets fired. I could never lose my job. Square girls are stupid and uptight. You should really have your own job.

I do think a pimp is better than a prostitute. He doesn't go around selling himself. My little brother was coming up to visit and I said, "Daddy, try not to act like a pimp around him. I don't want my brother to know what I do."

He says, "I tell my family what I do."

I says, "Daddy, if I were a man and a pimp, I'd tell my family too.

I'd say, 'Yeah, I got six girls and they're out selling it for me. All those bitches give me all their money.' I would say that. But to say I'm selling my body and after I get through selling my body, I'm giving the money away. No." I says, "If you were a whore and sold your body for money and then gave all your money away to a nigger, would you tell your family?"

He says, "No, I guess I wouldn't." That shows a pimp is better than a whore.

A graduated pimp like Daddy doesn't have nothing to do with his ladies' business. He doesn't come out and watch me working on the stroll. I'm supposed to make two hundred dollars a night, but he doesn't beat me up and yell if I don't. Sometimes I don't make any money for months. I get up, take a bath, make up, and go to work. But I don't make any money. I wonder why. I can always make money when Daddy's down to his very last cent. Then I work very hard. But if he has other money coming in and other girls working hard, I just don't try. I pretend I'm working. I even think I'm work-ing. But deep down, I know I'm not. I guess I just don't want to make money unless I feel Daddy really needs *me* and *my* money, not just money from his other ladies.

Daddy is not a protector on the street. He doesn't watch for us and he doesn't take care of tricks that might hurt us. That's not his job.

I can take care of my troubles with tricks. I met a guy I've known for a couple of years the other night. He's fifty dollars. He said he only had thirty-five and would I give him credit for fifteen. He's done this before, so I trust him. But even if he didn't pay me back, thirty-five dollars is still a good trick.

After he paid the cab driver two dollars, he didn't have no money left. So I gave him five dollars back and said, "You owe me twenty." I didn't want him going around with no money, and he'll come back quicker because I was nice. I had my real money in my pants. In my purse, I had a hundred-dollar bill, six dollars' change, plus the thirty I'd gotten from him.

When we got to my apartment, I went in the bathroom to wash

and something told me—something really told me to come out. He was in my purse. He jumped and said, "I went in your purse to get a Kool. Is that all right?"

I said, "Oh, sure." I knew he took the money. I didn't want to accuse him in case he didn't. I said I was going to have a cigarette too. I stick my hand in the purse zipper pocket and there's no money. He goes into the bathroom to wash and I put the money from my pants in the bureau drawer. He comes out of the bathroom and I'm completely dressed.

He says, "What's wrong with you?"

"Nothing's wrong with me. Get the fuck out of my house."

"I'm not going to get anything for my thirty-five dollars?"

"Thirty dollars. I gave you five back. Which I shouldn't have done. Not to you anyways."

"At least give me a reason for not being with me," he says.

"You goddamned thief. You know the reason."

"Thief? What are you talking about?"

I says, "Somebody stole a hundred dollars out of my purse. I'm not saying it was you. But while I was in the bathroom, somebody came into my house and passed you up—I don't know what you were doing—and stole a hundred dollars out of my purse. When I came out, it was gone. I'm very sorry to think it was you. I think somebody snuck in here."

He starts hollering. He says, "I didn't take no hundred thirty-six dollars out of your purse."

I says, "How did you know how much it was?"

"You said a hundred thirty-six dollars."

"I said a hundred."

"Well, I figured the thirty dollars I gave you might have been in there too."

"How did you know it wasn't included in the hundred?"

"Search me. You can search me. I didn't do it."

"I don't go through other people's things. It's just something I don't do. Maybe you never learned to have respect for other people's property. I'd never take anything without asking." I'm real mad.

"All I did was take a cigarette. I didn't have any on me."

"If that's all you took, you had no business in my purse anyway. You could have come to the bathroom door and hollered whether you could have a cigarette. I don't know what way you were brought up."

"How can you talk like that? You're a prostitute!"

I says, "You're the same fucking thing. You're a trick, aren't you?"

"Well, I ain't leaving."

I switch gears. I say, "Well, stay here. I want you to stay."

"What do you want me to stay for?"

I says, "Just stay. I love your company. Just keep staying."

"I'm going to leave."

"I don't want you to leave. You gave me thirty dollars. You may as well stay." Now I'm fighting to keep him at the apartment. He's trying to get out, 'cause he thinks I've got somebody coming over. Suddenly he runs out the door. All the while we're talking, he's trying to get into the dresser drawer. I think he's heard me open the drawer and he wants to get my other money.

After he leaves, I'm shaking and shit and sit down for a while. Then I open the drawer to see if the money's there. That fool—he hid the money he stole in the same place where I hid my money. The whole hundred thirty-six dollars plus my other money is there. He didn't have no money at all.

Guys don't usually steal from me. I don't usually steal from guys. I only steal if I'm with another girl or a guy has made me mad. Guys who have known me for a long time trust me. When they go to the bathroom after we're through, I can take ten or fifteen off them. If they've spent thirty-five dollars, that comes to fifty for me—my usual price. A lot of guys have been drinking by the time I see them. Their money is crunched up in their pocket and they don't know how much they have, so they don't miss a few dollars.

Some guys plain make me mad. They'll come up to me on the street and I say, "Want to come to my apartment?"

They say, "Why don't you come to *my* apartment? You scared?"

I say, "What do you think . . . I'm going to steal your money or something?"

They say, "You're not smart enough to steal my money."

Finally they come up to my place. They think I'm so dumb that I *do* steal their fucking money. But I feel guilty, 'cause they might have little babies at home. I also think if a guy pays more than he wants to—like guys have intentions of spending twenty or twenty-five and I talk them into spending fifty and they're nice about it—they've already gone over what they meant to spend.

When I fight with a guy because he wants his money back, or because he's a prick, I fight to win. I know I'm going to win, because I'm right. If he catches me in his pocket, I know in my heart, I'm wrong, so I'm not going to win. When I'm right, I fight to my dying breath. Like when a trick tries to hurt me.

A couple of days ago, two Italian hustlers drive by in a big old Cadillac. I ask them do they want to go out. I says, "It's fifty dollars apiece." They say sure. I suggest we get another girl and go up to my apartment. So we start to drive and they don't turn around the block for my friend. They just head north.

I says, "Hey, wait a minute. Let me out of this fucking car." I can't get out, because the doors lock automatically from the driver's seat.

He says either I can be nice about the whole thing or shitty about it. Either way, I'm going to get it. I get really mad. He tells me he's going to cut up my face, because I'm acting nasty and cursing. I tell him since he's acting so nasty, he's going to get cut up too. I reach over and grab the steering wheel. I'm going to smash the car into the wall. By the time I get the wheel, he's in control of the car. Now he's going to cut my face real bad. He slaps me. He's driving and says, "You don't know who I am."

I says, "You don't know who I am."

"You ain't nobody."

"Right. I ain't nobody. Nothing but a prostitute. But I've been working for four years, and I know a lot of people who wouldn't appreciate anybody doing anything to me."

He says, "What you're going to get from me, you'll never forget."

"I hope you get all the enjoyment and satisfaction out of doing whatever you want to, because, whatever you do to me, you will never forget it either. Believe me."

His friend says, "Let the bitch out of the car. She's crazy. She might really mean business."

By now we're all the way up in the Bronx and he says, "Now listen. We're going to a motel." I'm thinking I'll just run away. He gets hip to that idea and changes his mind. He says, "Me and you are going to get in the back and my friend's going to drive. Take off your shoes." I figure he's going to let me get in the back seat and fuck them shoes. I'll go without them.

I have about three hundred dollars in my pants pocket and twenty dollars in my purse. He takes the purse. I say, "Please give me my purse back."

He says, "You can't have it back. I don't trust you."

I play on him. I says, "Promise? 'Cause I don't have no money." He opens the purse and sees the twenty dollars and thinks that's all I got. He has my shoes and I start to get out the door.

He says, "No, you climb over the back seat."

I says, "I ain't climbing over nothing. I'm not doing a fucking thing." He starts slapping me and shit. I says, "I ain't doing nothing." I wasn't going to get cut up and have to fuck 'em too. So he's fighting me and I'm fighting him.

The friend says, "Why don't you leave her alone?"

I've never had any trouble with hustlers before. One hustler will respect another. The friend keeps saying, "You have to excuse him. A girl last week robbed him for six hundred dollars."

I says, "Listen. If you're any kind of person, you don't settle your arguments this way. If a fellow did something to you, you're supposed to shoot that fellow. You're not supposed to shoot the next person you see because he happens to be a man. Because I'm in the same occupation as other girls, I don't see why you come after me. If you're any kind of fucking person, you go after the person who did it to you. What kind of gentleman are you?"

He says, "Do you think by being a gentleman I got this fucking car and all this jewelry and shit? Gentleman! That's not a word."

"Then what kind of man are you?"

Finally I get an idea. I says, "Well, listen. I can't fuck because I just had a baby. I'll blow you right here." I'm shaking, but when I'm in a dangerous situation, I don't realize the danger until I'm out of it. So I'm saying, "Please just hold still. Don't hit me no more and I'll be nice to you." I start crying and then suddenly I grab the steering wheel and hit another car. Nobody's hurt. I start screaming, "Now you going to let me out of this fucking car?"

His friend says, "She's crazy." He unlocks the car and I get out and start running. A police car picks me up and they ask if I want to press charges. I says, "All I want to do is go home." They put me in a cab and I went to Daddy's.

I won't go with a guy who has a nasty attitude. Hustlers you can usually trust. But if a guy comes up and says, "How much?" I say politely, "Can you spend fifty dollars?"

He says, "Fifty dollars for what?"

I say, "Can't you afford it?"

"Yeah. I can spend fifty dollars. Catch a cab."

I say, "No. Forget it."

"Come on. Isn't my fucking money good enough?"

"Good night." Some of them come on like that. Wise guys.

A guy will come by, grab me by the arm and say, "How much?"

I say, "Nothing. Just let me go." He comes on too strong. If he acts like that in the street, no telling how he's going to act when he gets you alone somewhere.

Young guys are little punks. They think they're Don Juans and shouldn't pay for it anyhow. They usually give you a hassle. If they come in two seconds, too bad for them. Young guys don't understand that fifty dollars is for one time, so I try to avoid them.

I also try to avoid the cops, but they pick on me. The pross cop, Pete, arrests me every time he sees me. He'll be out there not picking up girls and I'll be the only one he gets. I can be standing with five girls around me and he'll say, "Kitty." He does it 'cause I'm with

Daddy. He likes me as a person, but he wants me to go straight and be without a pimp. Whenever I leave Daddy, Pete don't arrest me. As soon as he finds out I've gone back, he puts me in jail.

Forty-ninth and Lexington is Daddy's corner. He has about eight white girls standing there. Pete sees all these girls and he picks us up and hears us talking. Pete says, "Kitty, you want to make a call?" I say yeah. All the other girls say, "Tell him for me too." We be talking and Pete's thinking—goddamn. All these girls—eight girls— if they make a hundred dollars a night, that's eight hundred dollars in Daddy's pocket. And God knows how many he has over on the West Side.

Daddy always has pretty cute girls. That drives Pete crazy too. He wouldn't mind if Daddy had black girls—but a nigger with white girls who pay him too! It's bad enough for me to be with a nigger; it's even worse that I give him all my money, and it's even worse I have to share him with other women. Pete is really jealous of Daddy.

Actually, one of Daddy's girls went out with Pete. Not as a trick, but social-like. I know because Pete told me. He said, "Do you really want to get Jean in trouble? I'm going to show you pictures of me and Jean at clubs." He showed me letters that Jean had written him. They were in her writing and said, "Darling Pete," and "Love, Jean." I told Jean I knew about it, but she said Pete had given her two hundred dollars.

I said, "Pete didn't give you no two hundred dollars. He's got a wife, two kids, and two girlfriends. He can't afford to give no 'ho two hundred dollars for the night." I never did tell Daddy.

But my girlfriend Cindy gave Pete a diamond ring for Christmas. I told Daddy and he said, "I'm going to tell everybody."

I said, "Daddy, you can't. Because Pete's going to be mad at me for telling you. And he's going to be mad at Cindy. You're going to be jeopardizing your own money just to get a bit of revenge."

One time I got arrested and Pete said, "Get any postcards from Detroit?"

I said, "Why? I don't know no one there."

He said, "Daddy's in Detroit. Been there since Tuesday midnight."

"I'm going to show you how much you know. Daddy ain't hardly in no Detroit, Michigan."

He said, "Call his house."

I called the house and one of his wives answered: "No, Daddy is in Detroit."

Pete said, "Now, Kitty, I'm going to show you how much you know about your man's business. He'll be back next Thursday."

I don't know how Pete knows. He don't talk to Daddy. Fuck, no. It may be one of Daddy's girls. Pete is just into Daddy's business.

Right now Pete likes me and wants me to leave Daddy and go with him. He's been coming on to me. Me and his partner used to do crossword puzzles until eight o'clock in the morning in jail. Pete says, "How come you always do crossword puzzles with Larry? Why don't you do them with me sometimes?" Or, "I think you look nice tonight." Little things like that.

Sometimes we sit around the precinct all night long, because the jails are full. Pete will say, "Wouldn't it be nice if we went to your apartment, Kitty?" Why not? Who would ever know? We'd just go to court in the morning from there. At least if we stayed at my house, we'd be able to sleep in a bed. Pete jokes around. But there's something underneath the joking. He still can't joke me out of jail.

I hate jail. It takes part of my mind away everytime I go. In jail, I'm losing. I'm caught. There ain't nothing I can do about it. I can't use my head. I can't trick my way out. I'm locked up in a little room. The cops have more on me than I have on them. I'm trapped.

Last time I got picked up, I had to go to jail, because Daddy didn't have no money for bail. I've been in the House of Detention, but I'd never been to Riker's Island. I can't describe it. It was just horrible. They don't treat you like anything but prisoners.

You get word faster in jail than you do in the street. Every day, girls would come in off the streets and tell me what was happening. I knew one of Daddy's girls had run off. I knew Daddy was in Boston. One girl tells another and the story goes from floor to floor. I heard one judge gave a working girl twenty-seven thousand dollars' cash bail. She was just a street girl. A girl in for murder had seventy-five thousand dollars' bond, which means about five thousand dollars cash. For murder. The whore gets twenty-seven thousand cash. The judge declared *her* a public enemy.

Jail is the worst place in the world. We had to wash windows and clean the whole floor. Everyone felt sorry for me, because I was the only prostitute on the floor. Everyone else was junkies and two people were up for murder. We had to wake up at five in the morning. Ordinarily I'd just be getting home. The girls all joked on me. They'd tell the officer: "Poor Kitty. Ain't done no work in her life. It's bad enough the poor thing's in jail."

In jail, you have different dorms. They take all the butches and put them in one room—as far as possible from everyone else. Butches aren't going to mess with each other, because that's like two guys. The femmes are put at the other end. All the straight people are in the dorm. The officers can tell who is what by the uniforms we choose. I get real short uniforms and loafers. The butches get midis and Oxfords. It's all organized nice.

There aren't no cells in the dorms. Everyone has their own little bed and their cubicle. Some butches, if they really want to be with their woman, they'll act like they're femme. One of them put bows all over her hair and had a little short skirt. She made a choker and bracelet with some yarn. She looked really cute. She was in the dorm for a couple of days and said, "I can't stand this show." She took her hems down and got her Oxfords. The officer took one look at her and said, "How did you ever get in the dorm? You're transferred. Just look at yourself."

The girl said, "Oh, I just didn't have anything to wear so I had to take this dress." She played it off, put the bows back in her hair, and got to stay.

Pat came in with me when I was admitted. She wore drag, but I was so mad, I didn't notice. We got sent to the hospital together—to get a syphilis check. They can't put you in general population until you're cleared; otherwise you might spread something through the whole institution.

In the hospital, butches would come up and say, "Boy, you look sexy with all that long hair. Can I brush it for you? Please let me."

Pat would say, "Don't bother her." Then she'd say to me, "Kitty, I'm not going to let anyone bother you." I didn't realize Pat was funny. She got jealous when butches said things to me, but I thought she was insulted because I was her friend.

When we were getting transferred, she says, "Kitty, see if we can get transferred to the same floor. Then I can watch out for you." We didn't, because the captain knew Pat was a butch.

I was sitting next to my girlfriend Sara at dinner. I said, "Do you have any cigarettes?" She had a pack on her.

But Pat said, "Wait. Let me give them to Kitty." She put a letter in her pack. "Look inside. Look inside." I didn't know what she was talking about.

I went back up to the floor and took out a cigarette. There was a love letter inside the pack. It said: "I really dig you and I don't know if you knew. It hurts me now that we can't be together. I used to love to wake you up in the morning and take you to the shower. I used to love to clean up your room for you. It hurt me that I couldn't do anything, because I know you're not like that." She says she's coming to the gym tonight.

I was going to the gym to see my other friends. All the floors come at the same time. You play basketball, volleyball, and ping-pong. The butches and femmes sit in the bleachers and neck.

I didn't want to tell Pat that our friendship was finished because of the letter. I'm not prejudiced to being a lesbian.

Pat caught up with me in the gym and said, "Look at what your man did to you."

I said, "He had a reason. And because one man left me in jail, I don't think that's reason to turn against all men. But you and me are still going to be friends."

We're walking down the hall and she puts her arm around me. I don't think nothing of it. In the street, girls come up and say, "Hi, how are you doing?" In jail, they come up and kiss you and say, "How are you doing, baby?" It makes you feel better about jail.

Pat and I got off the elevator and she puts my arm behind my back and says, "Give me some sugar." * She is *very* tender-like.

I say, "Give you what?" I say it real loud and everyone's looking.

She says, "Don't disrespect me in front of my friends."

"You might think you're a man, but I know you're a bitch. Let go of my motherfucking arm."

She says, "Kitty, don't talk so mean. You're embarrassing me."

"You're embarrassing me. I have friends too. I ain't no fucking freak. I don't like no fucking girls. I don't care if you think you're a man or not. Let go of me."

She won't let go and keeps saying, "Give me some sugar." That night, she writes me again: "I'm sorry that I rushed you, because you weren't ready for this."

I write back: "I don't want to talk to you no more until you can act sensible. If you're going to rush me, I'm never going to be ready for that. I'm always going to like men until they prove unsatisfactory to me, which they never have."

The next night, Pat comes over and the same shit happens. I say, "Now wait a minute, Pat. If you don't want me to embarrass you in front of your fucking friends, let go of me now." She gets mad and slaps me. I slap her right back. She keeps writing letters to find out if I've gotten hooked up with another girl.

I was really pretty cute in jail. I'd make up with mercurochrome for blush and a regular pencil for eyebrows and eyeliner. I made eye shadow with crayons. I had people crowding me all the time and asking for sugar. But I didn't go with anyone this time.

If I've gone to jail for a week or two, I never tell no one around 49th. They'd say, "Kitty, where have you been?"

I say, "Took a little rest." It would be embarrassing to tell them I went to jail. I'd look like a smaller person. What am I going to tell these people on my block—the bail was a thousand dollars and it took two weeks to get out? They'd say, "You're a sharp girl and you should have a thousand dollars."

I'd have to say, "It wasn't me. It was my damn pimp." How can I say he had to get his Eldorado out of the shop before he got me

* *Kiss me.*

out. I just don't tell them I've been to jail. I'd be ashamed of myself.

I work all year round on the street. I work on nice days in the summer and spring. But I work in the rain and all through the winter in freezing weather. It's hard to make money in the winter, but I'd starve to death or go on welfare if I didn't go out. There I am standing—my hair's all frizzy, I'm shaking from the sleet, and tricks walk by real fast. They don't want to stop and talk. In bad weather, they just have to put up with their wives.

It's harder too, because the cops can catch you easy. If you try to run on the slippery sidewalk, you fall down on the ice and they get you. I'd still never leave the street.

I couldn't work in houses and bars. In a house, it's dull. You never get to say anything. You can't use your wits. In the street, I have to use guile and finesse with my mind. Once every two days I get in a fight with a trick and con him. I never know if a guy's going to kill me. It's exciting.

In a bar, you have to sit and talk to a creep. Then he might not go out. You can't proposition him in the bar. You have to wait till you get outside. All the time he thinks he can go for twenty. Fifty's my price and he don't go. In the meantime, I don't drink, so I can't get calmed down and accept talking to these guys. Also, if you get a guy in a bar and you give him a hard time, he can go back to the bar and complain. In the street, there's nobody to complain to. I can take care of my own beefs, so I don't need protection in a bar. If a guy is mean to me, I jump on him and throw him around. I'm not interested in revenge. I'm just interested in getting my money together.

On Lexington, if a guy says yes, we catch a cab, zoom up to my apartment in the East eighties, get down,* catch a cab, and zoom back down. I'm all through. Sometimes I can catch a date and within fifteen minutes I'm back on the street. Within an hour, I can see four or five guys.

Some girls work out of hotels. That's horrible. I always get fifty dollars. If I go to a hotel, the guy has to spend fifty, plus eight dollars for the room. So he makes me come down to forty to make up for the hotel and I'm ten dollars short. That means a lot more work.

* *Have intercourse.*

It's much better working out of my apartment. I say, "Can you spend fifty?"

The man says, "No, I usually spend twenty-five or thirty."

"But I have a very nice apartment—a big double bed and it's nice and clean." They'll spend fifty for a luxury apartment. A hotel has a tiny bed, no toilet in the room, roaches crawling all over the place, dirty sheets—all for eight dollars. I change the top sheet after every trick. We never get inside the bed!

If I didn't have to work on the street, I'd go out anyway. I'd just walk around and talk to girls and fight with the guys. Guys are going to come up to me—working or not. I'd just say some crazy ridiculous price. I'd talk to everybody and do nothing.

I see 49th and Lexington in my future. I don't think beyond that. Daddy would like me to have my own business when I get too old to work. But I want to be a madam. I don't want to leave this life.

ON THE STREET

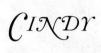

ON THE STREET

CINDY
a Streetwalker

RUTH [who works as a call girl in a hotel high above Lexington Avenue, as she looks down on the street girls from her window]: This is streetwalkers' paradise over here on Lexington. Every girl has a pimp. If you tried to work the street on your own, you'd get caught by a pimp after two or three days out. Pimps drive around and watch *their* territory. If they think you're working alone and won't join up, they'll think nothing of just breaking a couple of your arms. The street is dangerous and rough for an individual entrepreneur. As a matter of fact, it's impossible. I got into the business for money. I don't like giving a madam her forty percent. I could never give a pimp all my money! Those girls are nuts.

I do understand. At some point, everybody needs someone to love them, and a pimp can fill that need. A smart pimp looks for the girl who is alone; who has no boyfriend, no one she can rely on. He gives her everything she doesn't have—a place to sleep, clothes, something to eat. He furnishes emotional stability, plus physical comfort.

Occasionally, he'll pick up a girl who's eight-months pregnant and take care of her. But once that baby's born, the girl's back on the street. He convinces her she owes him everything and she's so totally sure he's right that there's no way she'll ever break away. These pimps have a strong hold.

CINDY: Prostitution was born in me. On the outside I'd say: I don't want to be one. But inside, I was always a working girl.* I lived across from the stroll in Cleveland. From my bedroom window I watched girls work and learned how a date was caught. At thirteen, I was wearing high heels and earrings—trying to look like a prostitute. I wanted nice clothes and the big Cadillac. All night long, the life seemed exciting. I began to think it was easy too; a girl would go off with a trick for five minutes and be back on the stroll again.

Working girls came to my mother's religious readings. They talked against the life: "What do you want to do? Quit school and grow up like me—a prostitute?" But I was a devil and very curious. Too curious. I was ready to be turned out at fourteen, but I was scared of my reputation. In the ghetto, everyone knows everyone. If any of my family's friends caught me trying to catch a date, I would

* *A prostitute.*

have got in trouble. All my mother had to do was look out her window! So I used to tell myself I didn't want to do it; it was wrong.

I'd been going with a guy in high school and, when I graduated, I found out I was pregnant. He got a job and married me. Then he said he wanted to come up to New York. I asked him how he'd get work. "No problem." No problem! He couldn't find a job, but he never did want one noways. So I started to work.* My husband didn't tell me anything to do. He didn't know. I learned on my own. I liked the work, but our marriage broke up and I returned home.

I took a square job in a record shop and Flash, the man I'm with now, used to come in. I'd heard tell of him since I was coming up in junior high. He was a famous player ** in our town. I was attracted to him, because he was in the life. I've always gone for flash.***

Square people look down on people in the life, but I think the life is elevated. We can make more money than other people and we're more honest with each other. A square husband is my trick. He's cheating on his wife. He doesn't tell her he's out looking for me. He pretends he has only her. All men are promiscuous. At least a player admits this. I know my man has other women. It's out in the open. Of course, square guys are fascinated that a man can hold so many women at once—and we all know about each other. At first, I *was* jealous of my man's other women. I was afraid he'd let me fall by the wayside. Now I understand I couldn't make the money he needs by myself. As long as he's good to me and respects me, I don't care if I'm his number-one girl. But I do want to be his favorite and I try hard to please him.

I work for my man. I couldn't have him unless I worked, but I also like the feeling that he needs me. Some women—like me—want to take care of a man—financial-wise, and also cooking, doing his clothes and housework, raising his children. I feel like a woman to my man. Because I do the work I do, he appreciates me even more.

Me and Flash love to eat. I go to the supermarket once a week. I try to get up early enough to prepare dinner for him before I leave. I do get off schedule when I'm tired; then I just run out for a sandwich and go to work. I do miss cooking dinner and eating with Flash.

* *Work as a prostitute.*
** *Pimp.*
*** *Eye-catching style.*

I start working early—at eight or nine. That's when you can make the most money. The cops don't look as hard until the rest of the girls come out around eleven.

I could work in areas where I'd never get picked up—away from the main traffic. But you make the most money where you're most likely to get caught—Park and Lexington in the fifties. Men come from out of town and stay in the hotels—they're the working girls' best customers. I do very well, but it's so hot, it's hard to work.

The pross cop, Pete, works from eight to twelve, and the other one, Larry, works from twelve to about five. You get to know the cops and joke around with them. They have a job to do and so do I. If they catch me, they catch me.

The other night, I went in the drugstore on 49th and Lexington to call Flash. I told him I was tired of the policemen riding around in circles and me running away from them. Flash told me to come home. Just then Larry walked through the drugstore. I seen him coming and tried to hide, but I couldn't. Larry comes up to me and says, "Let's go."

"Oh, Larry. Come on now. Give me a break." I start pleading.

"No, you have to go out tonight. I've seen you two or three times and I drove right past. Now you've gotta go."

The cops have to turn in a certain number of girls every night and, if they don't get their quota, I guess they get fired. Larry hadn't gotten his quota that night.

Pete will take you everytime he sees you, because he's trying to build a reputation. He picks up the same girls every night—trying to get as many as he can. Larry will give you a break sometimes. He may see you once and give you the eye. That means if he sees you again, you're going.

The cops know me personally. They see me out there every night and automatically know what I'm doing—whether I be doing it or not. I can just walk down the street and they pick me up and take me to jail. I think it's anybody's right to walk.

If the cop picked me up for "dis-con" * when he saw me talking to a guy and loitering for the purpose of prostitution, that would be

* *Disorderly conduct charge.*

okay. But I resent going into a restaurant and having a cop come in and take me out. Some plainclothesmen come up and snatch you. I don't even have to be propositioning. I don't have to say a word. I don't think that's right.

If they catch me at work, I don't mind going to jail. But it's money going to waste if I haven't did anything. I have twenty-two cases on my sheet * and only eight were righteous. The rest were for nothing; a guy came over, flashed his badge and took me to jail. I'd call that harassment.

Of course, I could tell the judge: "I didn't proposition him." But the judge won't believe me. He'll believe the cop first. To jail I go.

Jail is horrible. The matrons make you get all the way undressed and feel you up. Most of them are lesbians. They treat you like a number; lock you up in a cell, and in the morning you get taken to the bull pen at court.

The bull pen is filthy. I've seen mice running through. At noon, they give you a little cheese or baloney sandwich. You're upset. In all that time, you're sitting there and not getting your rest. You have to be back on the street that night.

You have to wait for your arresting officer to come and let you out. Larry gets you out of court pretty early. He's decent. But one time Pete picked me off the street at nine o'clock at night and didn't get me out until nine o'clock the next night. The cops get paid overtime. The longer they keep you in jail, the more money they make.

After you've been on the street for a while, you lose respect for the cops, because you see how phony they are. They be doing so many things themselves, and yet, they'll go out and arrest somebody else. I heard that Larry was messing with one girl on the street. I've never offered to go to bed with him. I'd rather go to jail.

The other night, a man took me to a hotel room and said, "I'm a pross officer." He showed me his badge. "Go to bed with me."

"Take me to jail," I says. "As far as I'm concerned, you're just a human like any other man. I'm not going to treat you any different. You're going to have to pay me. If not, just take me to jail. I'm not giving up nothing for nothing." So he paid me. Like any man does.

* Yellow sheet that documents a person's entire criminal record.

A lot of girls would have panicked and given him what he wanted. I don't think that's right. Cops are out there doing a job. If they're going to work, let them work. If not, I'll show them a nice time—for money. It doesn't matter whether he's a police officer or a lawyer. He's a man and a trick.

Cops anywhere resent players and their ladies. They bust us and harass us and figure that's money out of our pockets. One time my man got arrested. The first thing the cop said was, "I hate pimps and junkies." Cops don't make much money, so they can't stand to see someone else doing good. They try to get us in jail.

I'm good at what I do. Flash inspires me. I work as hard as I can for him. If I'm tired or not feeling well, he gives me a night off. He knows I don't make excuses. Some guys work their girls seven days a week—even on Sundays when there's not much business. I don't get a day off now, because Flash's trying to move up and it's hard for him to see I get tired after days on the stroll.

I like my work. It's not an ordinary office job. This business is exciting and it pays well. I try to get two hundred a night minimum, but sometimes I make as much as seven. We don't have a quota in our family.* We work till the night's over and get as much as we can. Some pimps set an amount for each evening, but that's not smart. The girls make their minimum quick and quit. They get lazy.

I could make more money working off the phone at home—away from the street and the police. Men I meet like me and I give them my number. I built up a big phone business. But when my little boy came to live in New York, I stopped giving my number out and changed the phone. I didn't want tricks coming in and out of the apartment with my son there. Often he stays with a babysitter during the week. But maybe Flash and me want to keep him with us. We couldn't do that with tricks around. So my phone business is dead and I'm still on the street.

Maybe my work will let up a little, because Flash has a new girl. She's white. He's had white wives before, but they only stayed for a day or two. I hope this girl sticks. Flash would be moving up. I don't

* *A pimp and his various women.*

know her well, but how could I feel any prejudice toward her because she's white? She's doing the same thing I'm doing. She has a black man and so do I.

When I was coming up, I didn't have any white friends. I had an all-black life in the ghetto. But the life's not that way. Now some of my best friends are white. Color doesn't make much difference in the life. We have something more in common—the same problems with work and the police; the same outlook on money and the law. Everybody's considered a person as long as they're in the life. I don't feel discriminated against—not inside the life. But outside, I still do.

The cops harass black girls more than white. They know a black girl has a pimp and that drives them crazy. So we go to jail more than white girls. Dates pick a white girl first, so she can make more money. I've heard some black girls say, "This date only spent twenty dollars on me, but when he goes with a white girl, he spends a hundred." If I'm standing next to a white girl on the stroll, a guy will choose her and come back for my phone number. He was embarrassed to pick a black girl in front of a white girl, but he *wanted* me.

I have to confront this outside world every day, so my life is harder than Flash's. He never has to leave the life. He doesn't get kicked out of restaurants. He doesn't have to go with square dates who look down on you because you're a prostitute.

They give you a hard way to go. You tell them not to pinch you and they do anyway. They try to stay longer than they're supposed to. They try to underpay and say smart little things. Some men don't like black women, or they feel guilty about going with black women. These dates are complicated. There are white girls on the street. If they wanted a white girl, they could have one. I think they punish themselves by going out with me. But I'd just as soon be black.

Flash spends his time with people in the life. Anybody who hustles is in the game or the life. That includes not only pimps and prostitutes, but con men * and boosters.** Con men can make fifty thousand in one haul. Very heavy money and very heavy time.

I'm not out robbing anybody and I definitely wouldn't want to go to prison. If a guy leaves his wallet in the hotel room, I might keep

* *Confidence men.*
** *One who steals clothes, television sets, and other goods and sells them.*

it. But I'm not a thief; I'm a whore, not a robber.

Flash knows all the games in the life, but he wouldn't go for them. I certainly don't want no dope pusher for a man. We have a friend who owned a lounge and had top entertainment. He had a beautiful home and cars and children—he was doing very well. Now he's in the penitentiary, for pushing dope. He'll be gone for the rest of his life. You build up so much, for what? Just to go to the penitentiary? Prostitution is nothing but a misdemeanor. The most you can get is ninety days. If you pay your fines, there's nothing to worry about.

I *am* tired of the hassle with the cops. I'd like to have prostitution legalized, but it would be hard to do. I make about seventy thousand a year. Some girls make very little. They could charge me twenty thousand in taxes, but they can't do that to a girl who makes ten. And how would they ever find out what you make?

Pimps would hate legal prostitution. They want all the money for themselves. Just as simple as that. Flash wouldn't like me to work for my money and then give half of it up to someone who does nothing—like the government.

I've never wanted anyone but Flash. I do want a nice home, some security, a car, jewelry, and clothes. I figure I wouldn't have to work so hard if we had money in the bank. Right now, we're saving because Flash wants a Rolls-Royce in the fall. Then we'll fix up the apartment and start saving.

I love New York. I have peace of mind here. I can do my own things and not worry about what anyone says. When I'm around my family in Cleveland, I'm tense and nervous. I'm always having to please them. They put so many demands on me. They're always saying, "Why don't you get a job?"

WORKING FOR A BUSINESS

WORKING FOR A
BUSINESS

SHERRY
a Graduate of the Street

SANDY: I met Sherry the first time I ever went to jail in New York. That was a bad night for me. The cops had picked up so many girls there wasn't any room in Manhattan and we had to go all the way up to the Bronx.

I was scared to death, but Sherry was just sitting there reading a newspaper. She'd always been a loner, because she's a very hard worker. Most girls on the street fool around— gossip and don't get down to business. Sherry noticed I was frightened and came over. She knew how to handle jail. It's just part of being on the street.

SHERRY: I don't think it's right or wrong to sell your body. It's your own body and you can do what you want with it.

What turned me on to the life was not sex. It was the flashy apartments and the flashy cars. The money is so good; the life so fast. I like being with people who are doing something illegal. I've never liked straight people.

My parents were middle class. My father owns his own business and does very well. I had an average upbringing, went to training school, and then became a secretary. I continued to live with my family in Connecticut and commuted to New York. I moved up to working on computers and made about six hundred a month—pretty good for a young square. Middle-class parents always want to make something of their children. Mine did, so I always got what I wanted. In that sense, I was not prepared for this life. It takes a long time to build up your money, businesses, and investments. You progress, but by getting a little now and more later.

I met Sweet. He wasn't pimping, but this prostitute was really digging him and she turned him out—hipped him to everything.* She started explaining to me what I should do. She knew I dug Sweet and he was going into the life. She knew I would too. Deep down, she felt I shouldn't. She said, "You don't really have to. You don't come from the right kind of background. You're not cut out for it." Most black girls in the life come from a broken family. Their background is not together. Their parents don't have anything and they don't care what their children do.

I may have been together, but I wanted Sweet. Sweet started pimping and I went out on the street. I got very excited about going into the life. I thought about all the money and what we'd have together. I was so happy that first night I went out. I was happy because I like money. Most girls who like money have to do this eventually. I was in love with Sweet and I wanted to help him.

I started walking around the stroll—very shy—and this guy came over to me and I said I'd go to his office. He was my first trick and wanted a blow job. I couldn't even do it. I got really sick. He said, "I understand," and he gave me the money. I didn't give it back. I

_____
* *Taught him how to pimp.*

just left. He said, "You look so innocent I'm going to let you go." I walked out. I'll never forget.

I had the guts to go back out and proposition my second date. He said he wanted to stay all night. I said, "Two hundred."

He said, "Okay." We walked all the way around the corner. I was very nervous because I didn't know where I was going. He was a cop—a plainclothesman. He took me in and booked me. I spent the night in jail and the next morning I was in court and paid my bill—fifty dollars. Your first bust is supposed to be dismissed, but mine wasn't.

I've gotten busted about eight times. The only time I really propositioned the guy was that first time. After that, the cops got to know me and just throw out the badge: "You're under arrest."

I always felt that part of the life was going to jail, but I also felt that I was a little too good for that. I never felt I belonged there. You're back to back with junkies who're getting sick. Everybody's pressed against everyone else and yelling. I used to just sit by myself.

Judges get uptight with the loud girls with teased hair. Those girls get five-hundred or a thousand cash bail. I never looked so obvious, so the judges gave me a break. My lawyer knew all the judges and the D.A., so he'd ask for a hundred dollars' cash bail or fifty dollars and the D.A. would smile and agree. I never had a rough time.

Not looking like a whore helped me in the street too. I used to make more money, because men prefer a girl who doesn't look like she's working. I don't understand why other girls think they have to dress like whores. It's their own hangup. In the beginning, they think: Wow. I'm going to work. They see all the other hookers with wigs and figure they have to do the same thing. It's not reasoned. It's just something they think they're supposed to do for "job security." Some girls actually think they look better that way. Maybe they don't have self-confidence. I did best when I wore my own hair, but I never went Afro, 'cause dates would have thought I was Black Power.

The street will wear you out if you don't take care of yourself.

You've got to eat and sleep; you've got to go to the doctor. Girls who don't like the work begin to look hard. I tried to keep smiling. Whenever I got fed up, I'd just go back to Connecticut to my family for a couple of days. With my guy, there was no problem. Some pimps insist that their girls work seven days a week, no matter what. They're disorganized and frivolous—always wanting money.

I resented the pross cops, because they discriminated against black girls. Larry never picked me up that much. I liked him. He was prejudiced, so I just tried to be nicer than usual. I thought that would make him feel guilty. He'd think: I really hate black people, but for some reason, I've got to like her.

I used to say to Larry, "I've really got to work tonight, 'cause I need money." A lot of times he'd let me go on working. He knew I had a pimp and the cops hate pimps. I've often thought they didn't mind the working girls at all. When I left my man, Larry left me alone. He came over and said, "I'm really glad you woke up. I wish the other girls would." He wished me a lot of luck. After I left Sweet, I worked on the street for three weeks; Larry never picked me up.

For three years, I thought only about Sweet, about being with Sweet and pleasing him. Everything I did was for our life together. I began to see the pimp's game—he gets all the goodies and you have nothing substantial. I wanted to start to build my own life and my own investments. When I told Sweet I was leaving, he didn't give me a hard time. He was smart and knew that I'd just outgrown the pimp-whore thing. I'd always known Daddy's girls on the street, so Daddy knew I was alone. He called me and asked me out to dinner. I knew what was coming. I said, "Come off it, Daddy. I know your line. I know the pimp's line. I really am through." We both laughed. He hasn't tried to cop me since, but we're friends.

I started working in bars and off my phone. I'd go on blow dates and stay for a couple of days. I made connections with these dates at clubs like the Pink Panther, where men in the Italian life hang out. Gangsters are very big spenders. Believe it or not, they're very intelligent and we'd talk about Vietnam and world events and Nixon, but we never did talk about what they were into—their business lives.

When you have a blow date, a couple of men come to your house for three days. I'd be a hostess—order food so we could eat and blow coke and talk and sleep. Coke keeps you awake, so sometimes you don't sleep at all. You just keep sniffing.

Men in the Italian life dig being with prostitutes, because we're all in the life—in different areas. I never treated them like tricks. A trick you see and that's it. I'd treat them like Johns—I'd pass the time of day. They're people and we'd have a lot of fun. Coke turns me off sex, but the guys still wanted it. I had to work hard to make them come, though.

The last time I went to a blow party, some guy said, "I really hate niggers."

I said, "Right on." At the end of the evening, he came up and said, "You're a nice person. You didn't get uptight about what I said."

I said, "Yeah, but I can't stand guineas." We just laughed it off.

I left the street just about the time the economy went to pot. Three years ago, you'd see a lot more pimps and girls out. The recession has affected business. Gangsters seem to have an easier time with money, whether it's tight or not. I've also been working at a massage parlor for money.

My friend Yvette said, "I want you to meet this date of mine, Leonardo. He owns a massage salon."

I went up and Leonardo took me to a room and told me, "You're nice. Give me a massage." After I passed that test, he said, "Whatever you do in the room is your own business." He went over ordinary procedures.

You show the man into the room and take him to the sauna once he's undressed. He showers and then you rub him down with lotion. That's when I ask if he wants something extra. I usually charge thirty for a blow job. It's a lot of money after paying twenty-five for a massage, but the men who come here want it real bad. I don't know why.

[Customer one enters.]
SHERRY: *What kind of cream would you like?*
MAN: *Anything's fine.*

SHERRY: *Do you live in New York?*

MAN: *I come here on business.*

SHERRY: *What kind of business you in?*

MAN: *I work for the Government, so I take trips.*

SHERRY: *What kind of Government?*

MAN: *Air Force. I'm a civilian in the Air Force.*

SHERRY: *Would you like oil on your stomach?*

MAN: *I can't hear too well!*

SHERRY: [Beginning to come on] *What do you do for fun?*

MAN: [Straight] *I fly airplanes and work in the garden and chase women and play bridge.*

SHERRY: [Putting him on] *How about chess?*

MAN: *I'm a lousy chess player. I can't think of what to move when. I can't think hard about more than one thing at a time.*

SHERRY: *I don't like to give a hard massage.*

MAN: *This is fine.*

SHERRY: *How'd you hear about this outfit?*

MAN: *Actually, my friend I come with, he heard about it.*

SHERRY: [Suggestive] *Know what it's like here?*

MAN: *Well, he heard about it in the paper. Of course, these places have been getting a lot of publicity lately. They don't give the addresses, but you can find them!*

SHERRY: *Anything else I can do?*

MAN: *What?*

SHERRY: *You didn't hear that one! Did you have anything else in mind?*

MAN: [Somewhat confused] *Just a good massage.*

SHERRY: [Doesn't elucidate] *Want to turn over please? I don't have any more towels, so I won't cover you.*

MAN: *I have liberated virtues.*

SHERRY: *What are you staring at?*

MAN: *You. You're attractive.*

SHERRY: [Again provocative] *I am?*

MAN: *You perform well.*

SHERRY: *So that's all your body you want massaged?*

MAN: *What else is there?*

SHERRY: *I asked you! I thought you just wanted a body massage.*

MAN: *I just want to relax. I feel undressed. I never feel that way.*

SHERRY: ⟦Frustrated and now direct⟧ *Want something extra?*

MAN: *I don't know what the extra things include. But okay.*

SHERRY: *French?*

MAN: *Cost more money?*

SHERRY: *Twenty-five.*

MAN: *I'd go for ten.*

SHERRY: *Twenty-five. I can't go for less.*

MAN: *I guess that's all for my massage!*

SHERRY: *Come back again when you feel like it. My name's Sherry.*

⟦Customer two enters.⟧

SHERRY: *You ever been here before?*

MAN: *Yeah. I'll just go shower. I knew Christina.*

SHERRY: *She's a lovely girl.*

MAN: *Did she leave?*

SHERRY: *I think she's still around New York, but she isn't here.*

MAN: *She gave me her number, but it doesn't work.*

SHERRY: *I don't have it. I didn't know her that well. I'll get some lotions. Like anything special? What have you been up to?*

MAN: *Working really hard. How about you?*

SHERRY: *Not much. Where do you live?*

MAN: *I got transferred to Rhode Island. I knew Christina when I lived here.* ⟦Sherry is massaging⟧. *That feels good.*

SHERRY:	*Did Christina ever do anything else?*
MAN:	⟦Naive⟧ *I don't know. I just met her here.*
SHERRY:	*I mean, do you want anything else tonight?*
MAN:	*Sure.*
SHERRY:	*What kind of arrangements did you and Christina have?*
MAN:	*You tell me.*
SHERRY:	*No, you tell me what you two did and we'll do the same.*
MAN:	⟦Somewhat shy⟧ *We used to . . .*
SHERRY:	⟦Direct⟧ *She used to blow you. And what did you give her?*
MAN:	*Ten dollars.*
SHERRY:	*See, I don't do that for ten dollars.*
MAN:	*Okay. What?*
SHERRY:	*I usually go for twenty-five.*
MAN:	*That's a lot of money. Let me check and see if I got it.*
SHERRY:	*I have to have twenty-five. I get that for french.*
MAN:	*Go ahead.*
SHERRY:	*You have to take care of me now.* ⟦He pays her.⟧ *You come up often?*
MAN:	*Not since I've been transferred. I used to. I like to meet the same girl. We get familiar.*
SHERRY:	*You want me to suck you off, right?*
MAN:	*Go down.*
SHERRY:	⟦Sucking⟧ *You're nice.*

⟦Twenty-one seconds without dialogue on tape recorder.⟧

MAN:	*You're too much. I could go two or three or four times with you, babe. Suck it. Suck it.*
SHERRY:	*Not again.*
MAN:	*How about twice? Got someone else coming?*
SHERRY:	*We'll go if you want to pay me again.*
MAN:	*But after what's happened—won't you go for fun?*

SHERRY:	*That spoils it.*
MAN:	*Then I've just got to simmer down.*
SHERRY:	*Stay right there.*
MAN:	*Can I stay?*
SHERRY:	*You've got to go now.*
MAN:	*Good things happen today.*
SHERRY:	*That's the only way to feel.*
MAN:	*See you again?*
SHERRY:	*[Polite] I hope so.*
MAN:	*Just ask for Sherry?*
SHERRY:	*You're really nice. It was nice to meet you.*
MAN:	*It was nice to meet you. Be a good girl. Bye.*

SHERRY: I don't give more than blow jobs here. Some girls don't do anything extra and I'd feel uncomfortable making noise. The walls are thin; they don't even reach the ceiling.

I think I had a cop once, but anytime I get bad vibrations from someone, I don't say anything. I'll just talk and give them a massage. If someone says, "How long have you been working here?" "What else do you do?" "How many people do you see a day?" "What kind of place is this?"—I don't like the guy. If he suggests I do something, I say, "I don't know. You'll have to speak to the boss." Then Leonardo comes in and checks his identification.

I'm actually protected in the massage salon. I wasn't on the street. I spent all my time running away from cops and playing hide and seek. Here, the boss can look out for me.

What I like best about my work is being in the life. It's everything I thought it would be and more. When I first started, I thought the life was limited to pimps and prostitutes. I'm out of that bag now and still in the life. That includes anyone who hustles—pimps, prostitutes, con men, and gangsters. It's square people I can't stand. I like people who can always figure a way to get something for nothing—or next to nothing. We all use boosters—buy stolen goods from them and get quality merchandise as cheap as possible. That means diamonds!

People in the life always have money and know what's happening. They're into today. They're advanced. If you're straight, you're going to go through life the right way and get things slowly. The life is a short cut.

Most people in the life are earthy people. You've got to become open-minded. You don't have to accept everything—like I don't dig wife-in-laws any more. I don't dig sharing my man, but I'm open to it in other people.

While people in the life cheat a little on the outside world, they're straight with each other. I have very good friends. I've always been uptight about being black with square white people. In the life, there's true integration. We may discriminate against squares, but we don't discriminate black and white. I mean that in the sense that you forget color. If you dig someone in the life, you dig them. Period. I've never been around white people like I am now. I'm relaxed. I didn't think I'd ever be able to relax around the opposite color—even at the same social level. In the life, color fades away into the background. The ties of the life are stronger than racial bonds.

When people in the life get together, everyone has a story. You learn by everyone's experiences. Like there's drag girls. A drag girl is a con girl who tries to meet old ladies. You take a girl like me— sort of a square-looking person—and another girl who's hipper in style. I might put on a uniform and play a nurse. I have an envelope chocked with money—about fifteen thousand dollars. Walking down the street, I pick out a well-dressed old lady who looks like money. I say, "Look, I just found this." I hold out the envelope and look real stupid. I say, "I just moved to New York and I don't know anything about the city. What should I do with this money?"

Now I find out if she has any larceny in her. If she turns around and says, "You come with me and we'll split the money," the game starts. It's really heavy.

We end up in a restaurant talking about what we should do with the money. My hipper partner comes in. She walks over to our table and says, "I'm alone. Do you mind if I sit with you?" Of course we say sure. Then we tell her the story. Everybody starts talking about splitting the money. In the meantime, my partner starts talking to the old lady about more money. She's got something going and she'll take the lady on as a partner. We're really trying to get the lady to the bank to take her money out. It's got to be a lot more money than I have in the envelope.

Finally, the old lady goes to the bank and withdraws the money. We tell her to put it in an envelope. She comes back to the restaurant and we're all talking about the big business deal. This is when we switch envelopes—she's so busy talking, she's not going to check out the money. If we make a deal, we get both envelopes. If we don't, we have her envelope with twice as much money as ours.

There's plenty of people to con out there. Good drag girls make fifteen to forty thousand dollars a time. To be a drag girl, you've got to be able to talk. You're always talking so the other person doesn't have a chance to think.

I couldn't do that. The money is great, but if you're busted, you get heavy time. I'm also not much of an actress. These girls rehearse the game like they're getting ready for a play. They're good.

Now I'm involved with a guy I met as a trick, Tony. Actually, I was walking on the street and his cousin came up and said, "You're the only girl I like so far. Come up to my apartment." He looked so slick, I said no. I don't go to gangsters' apartments, so he said he'd come home with me. Two days later, I had a date with Tony. Afterward, Tony told his cousin he'd met this girl with a beautiful apartment. He described a special round chair I had. His cousin turned around and said, "Oh yeah, the girl on 86th Street."

I started seeing Tony socially. We'd run into his cousin, but he doesn't look at me. That's all forgotten, but everytime I meet one of Tony's friends, I think, "Oh, wow, I hope I didn't meet him on Lexington Avenue." You never know. I do remember every guy I've ever been with. I wouldn't even estimate the number, but I never forget the face.

Tony is the first white guy I've gone with. I didn't pick him because he was white. He wasn't white; he wasn't black. He was part of the life. I could not possibly go with a square guy. I can talk square. I could spend a few hours with a square; maybe even a week. But to get to liking him—no. I've been around the life and I'm spoiled. I like the fast life. That's where my head's at.

At first I didn't know Tony was in the underworld. I liked the way he dressed. I liked his car. I knew he wasn't straight, because he didn't work that much. It turned out he was in the numbers.

Tony's been up to my parents' home. We all had Thanksgiving together and they liked him very much. I just met his mother. She thinks my business head is good for Tony. He's well educated, with a college degree. But when he graduated, he started hanging around with people in the Italian life.

When I started with Sweet, I was square and plain screwing was all I knew. Just screwing him became a drag. It was boring, because he never did anything I wanted. He was uptight about going down on a girl and that's where my head's at. I felt like I was with him and giving him my money, why couldn't he do what I like sometimes? In the life, you learn about all kinds of sex. With Tony, I'm beginning to experience the variety.

I really dig giving Tony a blow job. When I'm sucking him, I dig sucking him. I've partied with girls on the street, but I never really went with a girl. We always faked it. Tony and I swing. I'll get another girl and now I dig the whole thing with another woman. In work, the atmosphere's entirely different. Maybe it's my hangup, but I can only function when I'm with someone I dig and he's digging what I'm digging. I don't have to hide anything.

If I was to marry Tony, I wouldn't do this kind of work. But right now, I haven't been on my own for very long and it's important to me to make money for myself. Tony doesn't object generally. Now I work at the massage parlor and with a few madams around town— anyplace I can get business away from the street. I was supposed to do a party with twenty men. I told Tony and he got uptight. He said, "I dig what you're doing, but I think you're a little too good for a freak show. You really hurt me when you said you were going." I didn't bother to go. I care about Tony. He means something to me.

I think one day I'll be wealthy on my own. Right now Tony and I plan our future together. Tony has money and I'm getting myself together. He'd take care of me, but I've just got to have money of my own. Eventually, Tony and I will get a massage salon. I'd like to own something in Connecticut, 'cause that's where I come from. My parents have confidence in me. They think I'm going someplace.

They've never known I worked, but I've always dressed well. One time, when I first left home, they asked me if I was a prostitute. I wouldn't tell them. Now I talk to my mother and just say I don't believe in working hard; it doesn't matter where the money comes from. As long as I give my mother a hundred dollars when I see her, she doesn't ask any questions.

I'm going to work in Vegas for the summer. Tony will fly out to see me on weekends. I know it's going to be a scene out there. All the wealthy people sit around the table gambling and I bust in— everyone knows where I'm at. I ease over to a table and try to meet someone. Or I just walk to the bar and order a drink. Some guy will turn around and say, "Wow, you're out of sight." If he's an older guy, I say, "You should try to find out how nice I am." If he's younger, "You're out of sight too. We've really got to get together, but it's strictly business." An older man automatically knows it isn't just for fun. You don't have to tell him.

I just dig standing over a crap table and talking to people. In the fall, Tony and I will go to Europe for a vacation. Then I'll figure out what's next.

WORKING FOR A BUSINESS

Foxy

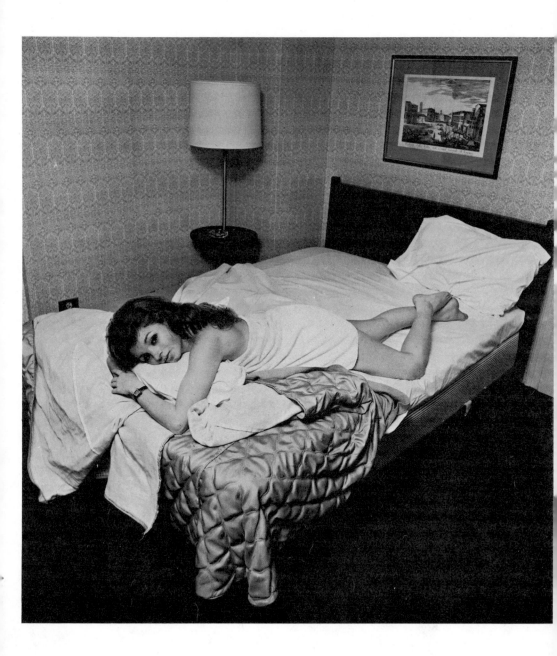

WORKING FOR A BUSINESS

Foxy
a Hooker

Foxy: There are different kinds of professional prostitutes. The tramp is the lowest form. All your girls sooner or later walk the streets—for variety, for kicks, for a change of pace. But the tramp, who only walks the streets—she's on the bottom of the rung. She's filthy, because she doesn't know how to take care of herself. She carries the diseases.

A girl who works for a madam or on her own, she's all right. Not that expensive, but clean. Somebody introduced me to a madam. She started asking about my business—how I did. I said I made out great. She asked about getting me some men. I asked if she meant on a business basis. "Yes, I'll get guys for you, and take a percentage of your business." Not on your life. I don't need a madam.

I am a busineswoman. I happen to work as a hooker in the garment center. I am employed by a manufacturer, who pays me, and *well,* for my work. There's no baloney with cuts. I don't give my money to anyone. I do my work professionally and keep the profits for me! Working for a business protects me—I'm out of sight of the law and my employer knows each man I see. That's the advantage of my position. And I always look out for my advantage.

Foxy. That's my nickname. I got it 'cause I could outfox anyone. I'm strong-willed. Stubborn. A conniver. Cute. Friendly. Lovable. I've got a bad temper. That's the worst quality I can think of.

Foxy: My experience began when I was a sophomore in high school. I realized I was getting spoiled at home. My parents had always given me everything I wanted, which was whatever anyone else had. If my girlfriend got a new radio, I wanted a new radio. My parents would say no and then buy me the best.

I figured I'd better get a job. Our school had an employment center, and they sent me down to the garment district. I was hired right off to work in billing. They didn't ask for my qualifications, but I did a marvelous job. The buyers would come in and, when they saw me, they'd pass remarks: "How cute" and all that. Everybody was always after me. It was a rat race. The big boss tried to put me in a corner, but no matter where I was, everyone found little me.

Then I found the boss; I got hung up on him. I let him know how I felt—by a look, a smile. He finally got up the nerve to take me to bed. I had never just walked into a hotel room with a man. But when he asked me to relax with him, I said all right. I didn't care. What the heck! I really liked him.

I felt funny walking into the room. After a few minutes, he took a shower. He came out with a towel wrapped around him and started kissing me. I felt embarrassed for him. He didn't have any clothes on. So I took a shower too. It took a lot of nerve. Then I wanted to go to bed with him. I really did, but I didn't know what to do. He started explaining. He taught me cleanliness. To be above-board. Not to be a slob. To have a good manner of speech. He set my mind for the business. If he'd told me the moon was blue, I would have believed him. The boss did this for his own pleasure. His partner actually started me working.

We were talking on a friendly basis. "Why don't you use your head?" he said. "Are you going to bed with a lot of men?" I was. "So if you're going to bed with other people, why don't you go to bed and make some money out of it?"

"When I go to bed, I enjoy it," I said.

"Don't be an idiot. Just go to bed with a few people and make some money."

Up till then, when I went to bed with a man, I really had to enjoy it. I had to feel, not love, but some kind of communication. The boss and his partner said I didn't have to feel anything. "It's a job. And you're getting paid for it." They kept repeating this. "You'll meet lots of interesting people." The boss had always taught me to be proud of what I was doing. "But don't get involved when you're doing it for money. Remain standoffish. It's not a personal thing. Say tender things. Definitely. To turn the guy on. Make them believe it, but *you* shouldn't! Put on a performance and keep yourself emotionally out of the way." I was so hooked on the boss, I believed him. At least I'd give it a try.

The partner took me to a hotel room and began to teach me. He showed me how to undress very slowly. Not all that corny sex stuff.

But with composure. With an air about you. Not snottiness. You've just got to hold yourself well. Then he took me to bed. He taught me the essentials of kissing. It's something you can be told, but it takes experience to get the full knack of it.

You start off gently—with a caress or two, and scratch your hand gently down the chest. Then you look into his face and turn slowly from the eyes to the lips. You close your eyes a bit and move in. This sounds phony as hell—like a love story. But this is what I do.

You work his mouth into an oval and then you kiss around the oval. You gently wrap your tongue around the inside of his mouth, and sooner or later, his tongue comes to yours and you can take it from there.

You caress his tongue and play with his hair and ears. I caress the nipples, first with my fingers and then with my tongue. The nipples on a man get very excited when you play with them, so I move down to the chest area and slowly toward the groin. I kiss around and play a bit. This is my set standard.

When I was sixteen, I had a great body. I was at my prime. I knew that men got the greatest charge out of touching me. But I worried about rhythm. You can have a great body, but it's all in the timing. I knew any woman could go to bed and move. But it's more than moving. Rhythm is nothing you can be taught. It comes from a lot of experience.

I found this with the partner when we went to bed. You have to be together. Togetherness. You can have perfect rhythm and all of a sudden give out or shift your body and lose that rhythm. If you break the tempo, you have to start from the beginning—or the middle. It's not as good as the first time. That's part of being a professional and I knew I wasn't.

I was worried that I'd chicken out. Right in the middle, I'd look at the man and say, "I can't." That would blow the whole thing. Or I might do something like hiccup or clear my throat. There he'd be—thinking of a beautiful paradise, on his own island, and katchoo, it's all over. I'd ruined it.

But both men kept telling me how good I was and how much

better I was getting. They built me up until I knew that if I had an appointment I could do it. If they thought I was great, then I was great. I guess I was a good pupil.

I was worried I'd meet bad people. Mafia types. You always hear about hookers and the Syndicate. How do you know what's going to come in off the street? But the boss said he'd know every guy. Would he let anything unsavory near me? No.

I didn't think I could make it with an ugly man. Looks mean a lot to me. I like to look at a good-looking man when I'm in bed. But the partner kept telling me that he wouldn't send me any creeps and I trusted *him*. He kept telling me I didn't have to feel anything. That was his job. That I'd meet lots of interesting people. And get paid for it. He kept repeating this and repeating it until I was brainwashed: I didn't have to care for a person, what good money I was going to make, and all the interesting people I'd meet, and how much better I was getting.

For a kid of sixteen, that was glamorous. I needed it. I still do. No matter how many men I have, a new one, who really digs me sexually, he makes me feel that I'm good and desirable and valuable.

I was in love with the boss. The boss's first love was his business. I knew I could help his business if I decided to work. So I did.

The partner lined up some interesting people. For me. I was scared stiff. I was scared I wasn't going to do a professional job. But my boss said men don't want a professional. They want someone who feels like their girlfriend. I was a girl. I had no special qualifications. Nothing different from anyone else. All I had going for me was my will power.

I walked into the hotel like a meek little mouse. Trying to hide my head so nobody would look at me. Naturally, my make-up was just so, and my clothes were very attractive. Little did I realize that none of these men were going to see me in my clothes.

I was afraid. I didn't want anybody to notice me. I didn't know what was going to happen. I wasn't sure of myself. But I wasn't so unsure that I wouldn't do it. I wanted to be good. Not just good, but excellent. I was looking for the highest possible goal. To be the best.

When it comes down to the nitty gritty, I was a bit worried that men wouldn't think I was the greatest. This is my goal and my achievement. Right from the start, I wanted every single man to remember me—never to forget me. It's probably a bad trait, but I'll do anything to get a man to the point where I know he'll never forget me. Like going to school. I will definitely not be satisfied with a *C*. I want a *B* or a *B*+. If I get a *C*−, I'm going to work my ass off to get a *B*. I know I can do better. I'll keep doing it over again until it's right. That's the way I am.

At the end of the first day, I knew I could do it. I put my mind to my work. I knew what was expected. I knew that working at it and concentrating and practicing, I'd get better.

I wanted everyone's head in the lobby to turn. It's that certain air you have about you. People are not quite sure you are a hooker, but then again, they're not sure you're not. You could just be an attractive girl that oozes sex. It was just the confidence. Those men had walked out with a smile ten feet on their faces and gone downstairs and talked to the boss. I'd get a phone call: 'You're absolutely great, fantastic. I'm sending the next one up."

I was tired, but when I received my money for the day, I felt so great. What an accomplishment. Look at this money. Me. Little me. Selling my body. I was good enough for someone to want me. All the girls in the office were beautiful. Their bodies were really tremendous. But I'd done this. Little me.

I continued to work in billing. When the partner had buyers in town, I'd work as a hooker. Buyers expect the merchandiser to provide them with a girl. It's a custom in the garment center.

The boss would brainwash a guy before he came up: "Listen, I got this real good thing for you."

"What type of good thing?"

"Well, if you're interested, come on over," the boss would say. "Because we can't talk about this on the phone."

"Is it worth my while?"

"You bet! Wait till you see this piece!"

I'd be sitting in the showroom when the guy came in. The boss would say, "Do you like that?" The man would nod. "Being that you're such a good friend of mine" [the boss made this all very funny; he's not too sad about the whole thing] "I'll make an arrangement with her and you two can get together." Three quarters of the time, the man would ask, "How much is it going to cost me?"

"It's on the house." The boss was very smart. He said just enough to keep the men hanging—so they'd have something to look forward to. By the time they'd get up to the hotel room, their tongues would be hanging out.

I'd go to the hotel room for the day. The partner gave me the room and floor number. He'd come and tell me how many people I was going to have, who they were—if they were good clients, I was supposed to give them anything they wanted. The partner would introduce me to each guy and then go downstairs.

Soon I developed a specialty. It happened because I'm a bug on cleanliness. I'd been taught to shower before every guy, but what about the guy? After all, he comes off the street—hot, smelly, and sweaty. That just didn't appeal to me. So I'd ask—soft-like and funny so the man didn't take offense—"Would you like to take a shower?"

I'd make it a game. I stepped on the edge of the bathtub and took the nozzle and squirted him right in the face. He'd start laughing and then I'd get in the shower and fool around. I'd soap him all over and turn him on. Most men wanted to do it right there, but I found that uncomfortable, so we'd dry off and go to bed.

Twenty minutes was my general time limit. To get rid of these guys quick, you've got to move—your arms, your legs, everything's got to move. I learned to do certain things all the time. Let's say the guy's on top of you. You wrap your legs around his hips and then move your legs up and down. This usually makes them come fast. You move your legs slowly and scratch his back. The main thing is rhythm. Keep it up for five minutes and you get that beautiful feeling. That warm, numb feeling that turns a man on. The rhythm is going precisely—scratching his back, moving your legs, your body. Everything has to go. You can't rest a second. You're an octopus.

About twenty minutes after the man has arrived, the boss would call so the guy knew his time was up. If the man was very important, he might get an hour.

I could knock off twelve guys a day—right from the very beginning. But I would not give blow jobs. If you do, your work's a lot easier. You can knock off twenty guys in half the time. It's also safer, because you don't cause so much irritation in your womb. But to give blow jobs, you have to have a very strong mouth, because your facial muscles get stiff. For me, it was too taxing. No one ever liked the way I did it. I guess if *you* don't like it, guys can tell.

I was very good for business. All the buyers wanted me. I was cuter and fresher and younger than all the other girls. I'd fool around with the guys like they were kids. I was a kid myself and we'd laugh and joke. Men don't want a hard-hearted Hannah. They want a nice, sweet, clean-cut girl. That's how I came on. But underneath, I was beginning to control men through bed.

One big buyer was giving my boss trouble; he was going to cancel his account. My boss couldn't find out why, so I had to pump the buyer for information. This guy would tell me anything if he was in the right mood. I had learned to relax him. Apparently the buyer didn't like the man who handled his account. No one had been smart enough to assign another representative. I tried to talk the guy out of leaving the firm—after we'd been together one day. He said he'd give us one more chance. I went back to the boss and told him to put a new man on the account. He did and his business was saved by *me*.

The business was great for me personally. I didn't have to buy my own clothes, because I worked for a clothing manufacturer. All I had to say was, "I need a new spring wardrobe," and go to the warehouse for an outfitting.

When men came to the hotel, they'd give me jewelry. It was kind of cute, because they knew the firm was paying me, but they wanted to leave something. I never accepted extra money from a guy—that's like a tip. I would have felt like a waitress serving sex and that rubbed me the wrong way. But presents I welcomed. I know I sold a piece of myself for those presents, but I still feel intact.

Sure, I had to be an actress and make a man believe something I didn't really believe myself. But when I acted, and when I lied, I compromised the *situation,* not myself. I wasn't totally honest with the men, because a man doesn't need that. A man wants to feel more manly; he wants to feel he's king. And he can't feel like a king if he doesn't feel he's conquering you. Of course, he's really not.

I was paid my salary directly by the boss. I got paid according to the number of times a guy came—twenty-five dollars a shot. Once a very important man came five times. The partner must have phoned eleven times, but the guy didn't want to leave. He kept getting me back in the shower and I kept turning him on, and he kept taking me back to bed. The partner got aggravated, because that guy cost him so much money, and wasn't that much in business. The more a man comes, the harder it is to make him come, so I really earned my money.

I could always make a man come. As a matter of fact, there's a certain type that I could detect when they walked in the door. All I had to do was rub up against them and they'd come—poor suckers. I could spot them—like Grandma Moses. You couldn't miss them. They'd look at you with such hunger. Like, "You ravishing thing. I want to eat you all up." I could see he was a sucker. He wasn't used to meeting a big-city girl. All I'd have to do was be very seductive— careful about the way I'd hold myself and lie down on the bed. Then I'd start to undress him. That put him at his ease. He'd worry because I'd have nothing on and he didn't know when to undress.

I'd just start rubbing myself all over his body. He'd come like that. Then he'd say: "Gee. I'm sorry."

I'd say: "That's all right." We'd take a shower and I'd give him the shower standard. That would make him come again. I'd tell him he was very virile. And he'd come more and more. I'd make lots of money with that type.

Most men really need to think they satisfy *you.* Once a guy came in and he was just beautiful. He wanted to do anything to make me have an orgasm. Well, this guy was really going at it. I was so sore I started to bleed. The partner came up after he left and saw the blood and went wild: "I'll kill him. What did this guy do to you?" I said I was getting sore. "Why the hell didn't you throw him out of the room?" The partner was all excited and called the guy the next day. He told him he was never going to get near me again. The guy apologized all over the place. He didn't mean to hurt me. He just wanted me to come. I told him I did, but he knew I was lying. That guy was really good. If I wasn't getting paid, I could have turned on.

Now when any man walked in the door he knew I was being paid and thought he was in control. I never wanted him to feel that I was controlling him. But I was. I was smarter and I knew what he expected. I did everything in my power to make him feel he was getting everything he expected plus more. That's why I'd tell men I'd had an orgasm; that they'd satisfied me.

Guys would ask and I'd say, "Yes, that was beautiful." It builds a man's ego to think he can make you come. Then he would come and, of course, I'd make more money.

I could never come when I was being paid. I was there for a purpose—not to please myself, but to please the guy. I was a hooker and I knew it. If I came, I would have been ruined. I'd get hung up. I'd let my barriers down. I'd have that warm feeling all over—that feeling leads only to bigger and bigger things. Business would have been over. I wasn't looking for involvement anyway. I wasn't searching for satisfaction for myself. Men have never been able to satisfy me unless I got involved and I literally couldn't afford to let myself go.

But if I were being paid five hundred dollars for an evening, I'd have to come. I'd have to get emotionally caught up. Myself. The man deserves something for five hundred dollars. He could have me all the way.

The more I worked, the more confidence I got. I didn't have to worry whether I could satisfy a man. I knew I could. Then I began concentrating on the men. They were teaching me. I studied their moves, their facial expressions. I studied them as people. Not clients.

In every man, I found a time when he became totally unaware of what was going on around him. It was his rhythm, his breathing. Most men are not slobs. They don't pant all over the place. But all of a sudden, they hold you tighter. They try to make you them. The rhythm's stronger. If they're kissing you, it's their kiss. It changes at the peak. If they're talking, they say, "Do you like to fuck me?"

I conducted myself as a lady at all times. I didn't use dirty language. One guy who I'd seen about four times, he said, "Come on baby, talk to me dirty." I must have tensed up, because he was just about ready to come, stopped dead, and turned red. And he apologized. If men wanted to talk dirty, let them get a three-dollar girl. I'd learned to turn a guy on without using dirty words in a disgusting dirty way.

Now fuck is a pretty nasty word, but when you're making love, it's toned down. It makes it nice. Sort of a whisper that comes out melody-like. Expressions have changed since I was sixteen. Now they don't say, "It's beautiful," but "I love balling you." It sounds crude, but it means the same thing. When I was making the transition from the old world to the new, I didn't like men to say, "balling." But now I know it means the same thing as "beautiful." These words are universal. When men are building up, they say, "This is really wonderful," and just before they come, they'll say, "I love you." That's very sincere—for a moment.

I noticed the way men came. Some come totally. They're really drooped and they've had it. They've spent their sperm. They also get this warm feeling—they're emotionally and physically satisfied. All men get taken care of physically. They usually remain hard afterward, because they've gotten so excited. They throb for a while. They've got to get a chance to feel emotionally spent. When they feel drained, they go down.

I found the closest moment is after orgasm. An emotion passes between you after it's all finished. That makes it more beautiful than sex. There's a look. Men look a little boyish. No worries at all. They're totally relaxed. It doesn't last for long, but long enough for me to notice how cute they are. No matter how unattractive a man might be, at that time, he becomes very attractive.

A true professional will get it over with one, two, three. She's very cold—so cold most guys don't want to be touched. They just want a blow job. She's just not interested in people. She shows no emotion and she doesn't care about the man's emotions. Just get it over with and on to the next guy and the next buck.

I got more involved, because I felt men needed it. Oh, I'd work fast. I could be an octopus—exhausted at the end of five or six hours. But, even though I didn't feel any emotion, when I was doing this act, I felt a man was trying to relay something to me. It was human to respond. I never responded to the point of love. I gave back warmth that he'd given me. If a man needed tenderness, if he needed a word or two, I'd give it to him. I tried to show him a bit of affection. But more than affection, I tried to give him a little love. Not what I call *love* love. That's lasting. But kind words and a nice, warm feeling.

If I could make somebody a little bit happier, if I could help somebody out, why not? You can see someone reaching out. And if you're anywhere near sane, you ought to know how to help—you ought to know what's right in this world and what's wrong. Men told me they usually didn't talk to a hooker about their families. They said most hookers don't talk at all. Even a kiss on the lips was too intimate. I let guys talk to me. They told me about their families. I tried to help. I'd stress what I felt was right. Like staying with their wives. I'd say, "Don't screw around with hookers. Don't try to impress the hooker so much. Try to impress your wife." [I didn't really mean it, 'cause I needed the business!] The guy would think, "Instead of trying to impress this dame over here all the time, why don't I do a little more for my wife?"

Maybe I talked to men, because I knew in my heart that I hadn't given myself to them as they had to me. Maybe this was my exchange. Maybe this was the way I paid.

The longer I worked in the business, the more I recognized different types of men. Eighty per cent of the guys I've met say they've never been to a hooker. But I've met every kind of guy at work—not just the sucker from the Midwest.

There's the little mama's boy who comes in his pants when he looks at something delectable. You can spot them. Some men are just typically Jewish. Their nose. Their eyes. The way they look at you, and drool at the mouth. There are some very nice Jewish men, but let's take a look at the yucks.

They're usually short and pudgy with the fat hands and the belly. And the little, little penis that is about an inch and a half at is full growth. I'm giving them a lot to say two inches. Put it all together and you have a conglomeration of a mess. It's very hard to manipulate in bed with them, because they're fat. You put your legs up in the air and you can't even feel him because his penis is the size of a normal man's head. He's highly excitable, and all you have to do is rub up against him, or play with his balls, and, oh man, he just squirts all over the place. He's in heaven. This is a type I don't like—pretty obnoxious and unattractive.

Then there's the Sephardic Jew. They don't want to be characterized with the American Jew. You can tell them, because their skin is a bit dark, not pale and real white like the American Jew. They don't have beady eyes; they don't have gooey lips. Their face structure is elegant; they're better built—taller, more handsome, more class and more poise. They are definitely not nouveau riche.

Sephardic men are absolutely beautiful in bed. They know how to treat a woman. They put themselves out a bit. They have control. The American Jew has no control over himself. Period.

I shouldn't sound so prejudiced. I have met American Jewish men who are fantastic. They're cheap, but when you get to know them, they treat you well. They like to put you on, but if you say, "All right, now you've opened your mouth, go at it," they don't know what to do. After the first initial shock of someone talking back to them, they take you up and grab everything they can get. These men love to be eaten and they go wild if you start playing with their balls. This is their bag. I really don't know why.

An American Jew appreciates good-looking women. He's good to his wife, who usually isn't so hot in bed. But he has a few girlfriends on the side. Jewish men never leave their wives, because they make the mistake of marrying Jewish women. Jewish women will grab anything they can get. Everything is under their name—like controlling interest in the business. If the husband decides to get a divorce, it's not worth his while financially. The man will just be totally poor.

Young kids are strong like oxes. You have to work your ass off to get them to come, and they knock the hell out of you. I had one kid who was twenty-one. He was going strong for two hours and didn't come. Meanwhile, I was breaking my back. I told the partner, "Don't send me any more young bucks." I had a full list that day and I had to use every trick I knew to get rid of that kid. Like when you're down on the guy and you've got your mouth on his penis and your left hand on his balls and your right hand up his ass—you've got all these things going at once. You're a contortionist. You end up standing on your head!

I did have one pleasant experience with a boy who wasn't even twenty. The partner asked me to break him in, but not to let the boy know I was a hooker. That boy turned out beautifully. He got hung up and fell in love with me, but all I did was enrich him. Now he's a better person and very considerate. I stressed that point. "Don't just do little things for me. Do them for any woman. We're not going to be here long; it can't last. But bring this to other women you're with." I was very happy about him.

I've met all kinds of European men. I can see why Hitler had a following with the Germans. German men are so methodical and aggressive. It's like World War II—with the marching up and down. Everything is precision. They come on strong, and then: bam, bam, bam—like a machine gun. I don't like Germans.

Hungarian men are something else. They just *luf* women and think every part of our bodies is beautiful. The toes. The fingernails. They leave no part of the body undeveloped.

I've found that European men have a longer penis than American men. They're not circumcized and that gives me a completely different feeling. I make love differently, because I have to push the skin down, so when I move up and down, the guy doesn't feel he's sliding in his own skin. Most of the men in my business are circumcized, because they're Jewish. They've had their little *briss* and the whole bit. I'm glad, because I like a nice, clean prick.

Besides being able to detect different types of men, I began to notice that the men who came to me were looking for something. They'd look at me and know that it was me, but some of them seemed to wish I was someone else—like their wife or girlfriend. They wanted some other woman to be with them the way I was. Their wife probably didn't pay any attention. With me, they could just be happy sleeping with someone who was attractive, had a halfway decent body and some talent in bed. Every man feels better with an attractive woman. It's a conquest for his ego. Especially for an older man.

I was getting a seventh sense about men. Through experience, I could detect a man's mood. If he was happy, I'd be happy. If he was depressed, I'd sympathize and pick him up. Most women don't have this sense. It takes a lot of contact to acquire. I'd met many men.

At my wildest point, I thought, why not go out and pick someone up? I met some marvelous men—but not New Yorkers. I tried the Wall Street district. The men down there are very drab—they have no color, no fun. They just maintain their business ways. I don't know how the girls on Wall Street can go with them, but someone has to. They go to bed like anyone else. They're just not my type—too professional.

After that, I tried working at home. A friend would suggest me or I'd get recommended by a customer. I didn't plan. I was just friendly and kidded around. I saw what type of personality the man had and took it from there. I'd talk about the girls he liked and then bring a little sex into it. This came natural.

I'd start flirting and bring our conversation to a more personal basis: "What did you think of me when you first walked in?"

I'd get his reaction: "You're a real knockout." "You're the nicest thing I've seen in a long time." "You're just beautiful. A real doll."

He'd ask me what I thought about him. I'd try not to say the bad things. Instead: "I think you're a real doll." "I think you're a lot of fun." Any of the clichés. Now we'd gotten on the intimate level.

We'd go out to dance. There's a way of rubbing yourself to make a man feel everything when you're dancing. He'll start rubbing me and I can feel him grow, so I rub back. Then I'll look up, "You're not supposed to do that. We're on the dance floor."

He'll say, "Yeah, I know. Isn't that a shame? Let's do something about it." That breaks the ice completely.

I hold him a little tighter. He's starting to climb the wall—literally. So I get alone with him—in a car and give him a few kisses and a quick rub here and there. That starts him boiling and then I get him to the quickest bed.

I started having dates for a day. I'd take a man around New York and show him the sights. I usually charged a hundred dollars for me and he picked up all the expenses. I'm not cheap. I liked to get him when the department stores were open. Then I'd say, "Don't you want to go to Macy's and look around?" He wouldn't be too crazy about that, because he'd know what was coming. But he didn't know how to say no.

I'd get him into the store and then start looking around. I'd say, "Isn't this gorgeous?" I didn't make it corny. I didn't come on too strong. I'd come on very mild and purry. Like a kitten. I'd say, "Gee, this is nice," and put it back on the rack.

He was usually a gentleman and had enough money to say, "Do you want that?"

I'd say, "No."

"But I want to give it to you." I'd grab my opportunity when I could. The man always paid.

I did refuse gifts—believe it or not. I once met a New York newspaper reporter. He wanted me more than anything in the world, so he asked me, "What's the thing you want most in your life?"

I thought about it—not long—and said, "A mink coat."

He came with the mink coat. I looked at it. I tried it on. I wanted that coat more than anything in the world. But I went to bed with the guy once and gave him back the coat. He wanted to keep me, but I couldn't think of sugar daddies then. One man couldn't take care of me—financially or sexually.

I got conniving. I was always looking for an in. If I saw a situation, I was going to take full advantage of it. To my benefit. I wanted to go shopping, but didn't have a car. I asked a guy to take me. He agreed. But it ended up that Internal Revenue was coming to check his books, so he couldn't go with me. He said he'd lend me his car, but that would have put a time limit on my shopping spree. So I got him to rent me a car for the whole weekend. He paid.

I'd get a guy to pay for my groceries or my taxis or anything I could if I was sleeping with him. Men paid for it, one way or another. I knew one girl who never paid for gas. She never paid for cleaning. Any time she could get a guy in the back of his shop, she'd give him a blow job. She rode around this city free of charge. She was quite well known in gas stations.

It takes a lot of guts to pay for something with your mouth. I couldn't do that. But my back—okay. I wouldn't hurt anyone or make anyone do something he couldn't afford. I just don't go near people who can't afford me.

I always had a full social life outside business. I never had any friends at work. To be in this business, you have to have stronger sexual drives than other people. A working girl has to enjoy sex. She needs it. That sex drive I had in common with other girls. But I didn't have friends because I couldn't find anybody with my personality. Other girls are too open about their work. I've walked down Broadway with a date and spotted a girl a mile away. Sure enough, she tried to pick somebody up. That girl is very crude. She has no finesse about her.

Outside the business, I had mostly men friends. My business sex life never satisfied me. I couldn't come when I was paid for it, but socially, I'd swing. When I'd go out with a guy, afterward he'd say, "Where the hell have you been all my life? You're tremendous."

I'd think, "You poor fool—you've just been given a workout by a pro!" Most men just thought I was terrific. Just a terrific woman.

I've usually dated about sixty guys socially. Sex is different on a friendly basis. I don't try to control the man. When somebody makes me come, we ball completely differently. I'm wilder and freer. When he comes, he comes totally—with me.

The first time I went to bed with Giorgio, he spotted me. He knew I was not ordinary, not the run-of-the-mill girl. He told me I was incredible. So we started talking. I told him I was in the business. He said he'd been a gigolo. I've seen Giorgio a lot, 'cause he can keep going for two hours. One night I came twenty times.

I'm not a nymphomaniac. That means, medically and technically, that a woman can't come. She gets that close, warm, numb feeling and then stops. So she has to have more and more sex in the hope that sometime she'll come. I do come. I come all the time. But I don't think I'll ever come enough!

I went out with a Hungarian engineer from a Philadelphia firm. Within the first half hour, he said, "You've got the greatest ass. I love your body." I knew this man would literally tear me apart. Over a glass of champagne, he said, "I want to make love to you now. I want you." I could have spit my champagne right in his face. There was no shyness; no decorum. But I knew the way Hungarians make love. Everything's out front.

This guy was no banana. He drove me crazy. He had about the largest prick I've ever been with. It was four inches in diameter and twelve and a half inches long. I could take all of him. I was getting very excited. I wanted more and I wanted it harder. I said, "Oh, baby, let me feel you." And I felt him, man. I made him come all over the place.

But I decided not to see him again. I enoyed him in bed, but he was a little too crude. I like them with all his sexual qualities, but with a more refined personality. I am particular. Besides, I found out he didn't like to spend money.

I had learned from being a hooker. Most men like to have girls people admire. It makes them feel more manly. If you've been a really good hooker, men notice you right away. Their heads turn.

Like my walk. I don't walk like a normal person. I don't walk swaying back and forth. I've asked people to describe it and I get such cute answers: "You sway with a bounce. A man can't stop looking at you."

I've learned to give men an honest smile. I've met more people that way. I'm not coy. I don't try to be a sexpot. Just a real smile. It's something a hooker's got that other girls just don't have. It comes from being with so many men. You get a sense of yourself and your best qualities. It comes from experience.

I've also learned to take care of a man. A man can walk into his home with dirt piled up high and he couldn't care less, just as long as you take good care of him sexually. The way to a man's heart is not through his stomach, believe me.

Professional women make other women jealous. They snicker. They look down on you. The suburban housewife is so black and white. There's no gray. But every day, hundreds and hundreds of husbands get helped by a professional. Half of these housewives don't have a head about a man's business. The professional girl knows something about business, because she's a businesswoman herself. She can give a guy the feeling that she cares. A guy can tell his problems to her. Even when he's wrong, the professional will tell him he's right. Sooner or later, he'll work out the right solution. I give a man understanding and a closeness that he's lost with his wife. With me, it's not the same old routine; it's a challenge. I'll talk to a man about anything. I make him feel he's king.

A wife won't do that. She's bound to say wrong things and degrade her man. I do tell men to keep up with their wives too. If she enjoys all those boring social organizations, he's got to ask her about them once a month. Not every week, because some of these women belong to fifteen thousand organizations. But a man's got to recognize that his wife is a human being and not just there to wait on him hand and foot. In turn, she's got to realize that he's not just there to make money so she can go blow it on furs and diamonds. I'm very complex about these things. I'm sure I've saved hundreds and hundreds of marriages. I care about marriage! It's bound to happen to me.

Society still looks down on prostitution. They think it's bad that women sell their emotional selves. After a number of years of selling, you do lose your old personality. You change and accommodate to fit selling—your body.

Men have to sell too. My boss sold the firm and his product, which didn't happen to be sex. But he still had to sell himself as a person. If he wanted people to buy his goods, he had to be personable and witty—whether he felt like it or not. One way or another, people in any business sell themselves. Why shouldn't a woman? It amounts to the same thing. I have never met anyone who's compromised himself so much that he's become corrupted, cheap, and just plain no good.

Hooking hasn't hurt me. It hasn't hurt my personal life. I could always separate them. A lot of prostitutes enjoy themselves. Not all of them do, 'cause this is a business like any other business.

The professional hooker does her business and becomes what she does. It's a matter of assimilation. Just doing it and falling into a pattern until it becomes a set way. It's not destructive if you fall into a good pattern. If you meet low-class people all the time, you cannot maintain high standards. If you lose your morals and standards, and you settle for anything, that's bad. I've always been involved with high-class people, so I act high-class. My background is high-class.

One night I called my father and said, "I'm going out tonight."

He said, "How're you getting home, because I want you to stop off and get some pastries."

So I said, "What, are you crazy, pop? I'm going out."

"Where are you going out?"

"To Boston. For dinner."

"Why are you going to Boston," he asks.

"I want a change of scenery."

"You want a change of scenery? I'll take you to a restaurant and paint a mural on the wall."

"But I feel like meeting new people, pop."

"So, I'll bring my friends."

"No, I'm going to Boston to have dinner."

So he wants to know who this man is and what he does. He wants to have his whole status in front of him. "Can I trust the guy?"

I says, "What do you want to know for? *I'm* going out with him." Then he starts laughing.

Pop says, "My daughter. There's no one like you." Pop was an altar boy and I know he's thinking: "Oh, God. I was an altar boy and I was a good kid when I was little. What did I do to deserve this?" But he keeps cracking up.

When I got home in the morning, I called him. He says, "What time did you get in?" I told him I'd missed the shuttle and stayed over. He says, "Where did you sleep?"

"I stayed in a hotel."

"By yourself?"

"Of course by myself—who else?"

One time I told my father I was going to live with somebody. He said he would disown me if I did. So that ruined that. All these years, I think my father's kept my morals up. I certainly don't think my professional life has affected my standards.

My parents don't know I was a hooker. They'd be completely shattered. It would break their hearts. They could accept it in someone else, but not in their own child. For me, it was always two different worlds. Being a hooker was what I wanted to do professionally. It had nothing to do with my family and my home life. If I wanted to be a hooker, fine. But nobody else was going to know but me. It was a separate part of me. I never lied to my parents. They didn't ask and I didn't offer. I've always hated lying.

If I find out someone has lied to me, I give him a lecture: "What do you want? Want me to think you're something that you're not? Are you trying to impress me?" If the man is attached to me, I make him feel so bad about putting me on that he doesn't do it anymore.

In the business, I did have to act. I had to lie. But that was the situation. I didn't want to get involved with the men, but knew that they wouldn't be happy unless they thought I was. So I'd say: "I love you. I came." I'd say it so men would believe me. That was part of what I was paid to do. Men lie in business. Why couldn't I? It's just the American way of work. I still have my standards and my morals.

Some people say that men shouldn't have to pay for it, but they do, one way or another. If a guy's married, he pays for it for the rest of his life. He pays more dearly, in aggravation and heartache. Plus money. When a guy goes to a professional, he gives her a certain amount of money and that's it. No involvement, no hangups, no aggravation. All women, not just professionals, get paid for putting out—one way or another. You're always going to have fanatics who feel that it's wrong, but they tolerate prostitution because it's needed. "Somebody has to take the maniacs off the street." Maybe if the venereal-disease rate gets high enough and the abortion rate zooms up, the laws on prostitution will be changed.

I've never had any trouble with the law. I've gone out with a couple of cops for my benefit. I used to see a detective from Queens. He handled prostitution. If I ever got in trouble, he'd get me out.

A girl's a sucker if she can't handle a cop. If the cop is fatherly, you can start to cry and say you have a couple of kids and no money. Say you're sorry and if you get caught, you'll be ruined. Give him a sad story. This is for the older, daddy type.

If the cop is young enough, just lay it straight on the line. "Look. Don't be ridiculous. I can make it worth your while." If that doesn't work, you've got your last resort. You can cut him in. But that is your *last* resort.

The politicians and law-enforcement officers would lose so much money if prostitution were legal that I don't think they'd do it.

I'm a modern woman. I favor legal prostitution. I also take the Pill. The Pill has changed everything. All the nineteenth- and eighteenth-century ideas, and maybe all the ideas since Eve put the grape leaf on, are falling apart. People used to be very religious-minded. Religion was their social diet. In the Bible, adultery was one of the Ten Commandments. Religions taught that anyone who committed adultery was a sinful person. The roaring twenties was a breakthrough. People started to be more open about sex and prostitution. Today, women have more rights.

In thirty or forty years, everybody will be going to bed with everyone else. You won't have prostitution. If you want to sleep with someone, you will. Hippies are the deviant group right now, but they've been contributing a lot, because their generation is the future. The hippies are freer about love, and their own children will be even more free. Each generation passes a heritage to its children. Eight generations from now, it's going to be free love. No one will buy it and you won't be able to sell it.

Right now, being a hooker is not ordinary work. I've liked the fun; I've enjoyed meeting different personalities. But if you're smart as a hooker, you realize you can't go on forever. Your body can't take it. The work is very demanding. A lot of times, I just don't want to go to bed with any old man off the street. I said to myself—what the hell am I doing here? Why don't I go find a nice guy and get married. I'll give him what I'm giving everyone else.

So I got married. My husband had blond hair and blue eyes. Just what I always wanted. But he didn't have a cent. I bought all our furniture with my money. To live the way I wanted to, I used up all my savings and sold my stock. Finally, I had nothing left but a husband and two children. I started working again—off and on. My husband thought I had some money left. But one day he found out I'd been in the business and he turned crazy. He wouldn't let me go to the supermarket alone. I had to leave him. I had nothing and started from the beginning again.

With children, I decided I'd better have a regular job, so I worked as a secretary during the day. That covered my expenses. In my social life, I'd get my dates—who didn't pay to sleep with me—to pay for everything else: the babysitter, the dry cleaning, the phone—whatever bills I had to meet.

Now I've got friends all over the world. People pass my number along. I get calls from people I don't know. "What are you doing tonight? Can I take you out for a drink?" I get passed on by recommendation. Just as a friend. No one knows what I did. A guy says, "You've just got to call Foxy, because you'll be proud to go out with her." As soon as they meet me, they ask me to dinner. I've been fortunate. I'll fly to Boston or Washington for the evening. The guy pays for the flight and the baby sitter, dinner and dancing, and a little extra for me. They never turn out to be one-night stands.

I've also been meeting guys on the phone. One guy called and he'd gotten the wrong number. I started fooling with him and we made a date for lunch the next day. So up pulls this beautiful Cadillac and a very tall man who owned four wig shops. We had a nice lunch and, the next time I saw him, he had a wig for me.

Another man was calling an insurance company when he got me. He'd just bought a new Eldorado and wanted it covered. I told him he had the wrong number and how sorry I was. He says, "You sound kind of cute." We made a date and he turned out to be a real winner. He gave me a ring. It's real rewarding picking up men on the phone.

I've decided I'm never going to be at the bottom again. That's why I'm looking for a man with money to marry. That might sound base. It might sound like I'm just out for money. Well, I am. I want money and love, but I have to have money. I have a certain standard of living. I want good things. Today I spend everything. I've got some money in the bank, but nothing to speak of. I spend it now. What the hell. When I get married, let my husband take care of me with money.

I do think I should marry while I can still have an exciting sex life. After a certain age, you can only think about what *was*. Sex doesn't go completely out, but it diminishes. You don't feel bad when it happens, if you have nice things to look back on.

You also want to be able to enjoy your kids. I have two. I'd like more. A woman isn't a woman without children. Right away you can tell the difference between a woman who's had children and a woman who hasn't. A woman with children is not like laying on a hard board. Men say my stomach's like a downy feather. Something you can snuggle into. I have softer, more pliable breasts. I'm more loving and affectionate. Men need this too. Men have actually preferred me since I had children. They liked me when I was younger, because I was a crazy kid, but they like me more now—mature.

I also think it works out better when they don't pay for sex. Men don't like to feel that they have to pay you to go to bed with them. Every man I see helps me with my bills and gives me presents. I've done very well on men.

Through my job as a secretary, I got a really good offer in an advertising agency, so I decided to make a career for myself. The head of the firm made me assistant to the president, so I run the whole office. My salary quadrupled. It's a wonderful job, because I meet so many men with money. I can combine sex and money and use my feminine wiles.

Of course, most women in advertising are oldish and they've lost their charm. That's not me. You've really got to have a sharp mind to play this game with clients. I do. And I have other advantages!

I met one attorney who often works for our firm. One night, we went to the Arabian Nights. We were joined by another man and his girl—she came in a bit late. My date was kissing me in the booth and turning me on when this girl walks up—very pretty, pleasant, and sweet. We were drinking and dancing—she liked me and I liked her. We ended up in her apartment and I was feeling no pain, because I'd been drinking screwdrivers like they were water. One thing led to another and we undressed. The four of us got in bed. She started with my date; I was with hers. We were at it for about four hours, until I finally felt a different set of hands on my body. It was the girl. She was rubbing me. I'd never had a girl touch me. I looked at her, she looked at me and we didn't say anything. This guy was eating me and she's kissing my breasts. Let me tell you, I made love for ten hours. When I woke up the next day, I told her she was the first woman that had ever touched me. She said it had been the right environment, that she really cared for me, she loved men, but if a woman came along, she knew how to appreciate her too.

These guys went crazy watching us. I said to my date, "What do you think of me now?"

He says, "I don't know how to tell you this, but watching two women make love to one another—I think it's so beautiful."

I said, "Doesn't it turn you off—watching us? Two girls together?"

"No. It gets me excited. It turns me really on."

Afterward, we went out and the guys bought us leather Gucci outfits. Men do pay.

Now I've tried my first woman, I'm getting more experimental. One night I wound up with two guys and me. Both of them were good. What one lacked, the other had. One could eat me and the other could ball fantastically. I don't know how it happened, but I went crazy. It was sex from all over the place. You feel like you have fifteen million trillion sensations going on. I've been to bed with guys who send me. But I'm still in bed. This time, I was up in the stars, floating. That was real ecstasy. That's how high I was on sex. I felt so special. So unique. A present just for passion. A piece of magnetic merchandise.

There's an account executive who's young and good-looking. He makes love to me on the stairs. He gets a tremendous hard-on. Then I say, "Take me out." But we just don't have time. Every night is filled up for me. I have to solicit business during lunch hours and after hours—any time I can get. So we haven't had a chance to be together—except on the stairs.

One time, I gave him such a tremendous hard-on, his pants got wet. He had to walk all the way back through the office with stained pants. He was embarrassed, but he made it. I said, "This is ridiculous. We're just going to leave the office one day and drive to the shore and make love all afternoon." This man has money and possibilities.

One of the account executives I work with took me out and got really drunk. He said, "You were a hooker, weren't you?"

I could have said, "What? Are you out of your mind? Are you crazy? What do you take me for? I'm insulted." But him. I looked him straight in the eyes and said, "Yes. How did you know?" I knocked him off his chair.

He said, "With a rear end like yours and your walk and just the way you know how to handle men. It comes from a lot of experience. How about going to bed with me?"

"You're my friend. I wouldn't go to bed with you for money."

He said, "I don't want you to screw me for business. I want you to screw me for pleasure." He offered to set me up as a madam, but I prefer advertising right now. I have a straight front and the same financial opportunities.

I do have a tremendous following. Last week, I went to a dinner party given for the agency's clients at the Waldorf Astoria. It was wall-to-wall men. When I got introduced to people, I oversold every-one on the agency. Most women in business are so drab they can't make an easy sell.

I've learned something too about these square business types. They may wear pin-striped suits and vests. But take these men out of their clothes and put them in bed—they really surprise you. They swing with money too.

I go out with a fifty-two-year-old lawyer. The other night, we went to dinner in the Village and we were passing a store and I said, "Oh Jesus, isn't that nice?" We walked through Washington Square Park and, on the way back, stopped at the window and he said, "Come in. I feel like buying something for you."

I said, "You don't have to buy me anything." 'Cause this guy gives me money right and left. I don't ask for the money. He just gives it to me.

One day I called him up, because I was buying stock and didn't have enough collateral. I said, "Could you lend me some money?"

He said, "Sure. How much do you want?"

"Seven hundred dollars." I got it the next day. Special Delivery. That was really wonderful. I don't even have to hustle any more.

BUSINESS WOMEN IN A
WORLD OF PLEASURE

DIANE

BUSINESS WOMEN IN A WORLD OF PLEASURE

DIANE
a New Madam

DIANE: Luck started me out in this business. I'd lived with a madam—as her friend. I happen to prefer women and she was my lover at the time. In addition to being around the business, I'd actually run her house. When we split up, I moved out and started selling pornographic films—picking up a little money here and there. But I needed to make more money and setting up a house was a logical choice.

I'd met a bar owner through a girlfriend. We went out, but there came a time when I had to tell him that I don't like men. Talk turned around to the business and he said, "Why don't you get into it? You don't have to go with people yourself. Just madam. I can send you guys." It seemed like a good idea. I'm happy when I'm making money and I can't take working for someone else. So I began.

DIANE: My business is like any other business. My office is my home, my employees are call girls. I expect from my workers what anyone else expects—loyalty and a good effort.

I worry about cash flow—about meeting my bills and how much money is coming in. I watch the stock market—this affects my business more than anything else. My customers either work for the Exchange or they're heavy investors. When the market's bearish, I have to hole up and wait.

I have to stay ahead of the competition. Let's say a John gets laid three times a week. He comes to me once and goes to two other madams. Now, I have to develop a gimmick that's going to get him here three times a week. Right now I'm having green stamps printed. A man gets a stamp for every time he goes. For five stamps, he'll get a pornographic picture; for ten, a magazine; and for fifteen, a free lay. Now, instead of going to another madam, he'll see me all three times, because he's getting a little something extra. Same as any other business—gimmicks and the quality of the merchandise. You do have to have nice girls. I get away with okay girls if I can. If I can't deliver anything but the best, I have the best.

Myself, I like gay girls. They're together and in touch with themselves. The men don't mean anything to them. They don't hate men; to hate, you have to love. They feel neutral: he's a nice guy, I'm taking his money and that's it. Gay girls think about something else while they're screwing. But they do try to give a man a good time. The other girls get too involved with their emotions.

We are supposed to be selling sex—and just sex. It's very hard for a straight girl to keep herself emotionally separated. The business disgusts you with men. You see a man at his weakest point. People tend to think of men as big and strong, but here you see them as little fools over a piece of ass. A girl begins to feel like a commodity; like she's not a real person—just an object for pleasure. She gets paranoid. She doesn't believe anyone can love her. If she meets a nice person outside the life, a person that really does love her, she pushes him away. Rejects him.

A gay girl can keep her emotions separate. I'm gay, so I know. A square girl who has a square boyfriend who loves her can also stay sane. She gets her money and quits. Most of my girls are either gay or square-with-boyfriends. I like to have stable people around.

When I built up the business so I could afford an apartment of my own, I got a square backer, who advanced me money to start this operation. He gave me five thousand dollars, to be paid back with a twenty-percent interest. It was more or less a favor. I paid it back in six months with no interest at all.

I got an apartment through an ad in the paper. It was a lucky mistake. When I came to the building, I talked to the super and he said, "I don't mean to insult you, but you sound like a madam. And, if you are, it's a very cool management. Lots of people in your line of business live here. Entertainment can be worked out. You can get busted every day and not have to worry about eviction notices." Every Friday, at three o'clock, I send a girl to the owner and one to the super. I pay the girls their cut—twenty-five dollars, which is fifty-fifty on a fifty-dollar trick. It's nice to be in a building with people in the life. You have your own little army. In a place with square people, you feel weird. Even if they don't know what you do, you avoid them. They're different.

Nobody knows my name. The apartment and all my papers are under my professional name. The papers are stolen—but there are two kinds of stolen. Some papers are lifted from purses, but then you don't have a choice of names. My people lift forms out of offices. That way I can use the name I want. It's legal, registered; it just needs a name I choose. I don't have five different names on paper.

Needless to say, I have very reputable references—square people I can use for recommendations. Because I happened on a nonsquare building, I didn't have to use these for the apartment. But when I opened my bank account, I did. I have one reference who's worth eight million dollars, so I can have what I want.

By the time I moved into the apartment, I'd accumulated some good lists of names. I had friends at health clubs and private clubs who'd give me their membership lists. I got a five-thousand-name list of celebrities in television and movies—their private numbers. No madam in New York has these numbers. I haven't had to pay for lists, but usually you do.

I first sent out an announcement: "Diane Lilly, Public Relations, is opening a plush new apartment." At the top of the card, the name of the company: "Lilly and Company, Public Relations." Most guys who get that invitation know exactly what I have in mind. The ones who don't call back, I call eventually. If I understand by the conversation that they would be offended, I can switch around to a legitimate tack and get off.

When a man calls, I tell him I have a penthouse and lovely young ladies—a unique type of public relations. I wait to see how he responds. Once I got through telling a square guy about the penthouse and the girls and he said, "Yes, but what's Lilly and Company?"

I says, "Well, dear, ladies of the evening. If you perhaps want to spend some time with a young lady, and you liked her and after a while wanted to go to bed with her, for a certain price, you could."

I had one wife call. She's cursing me out and says, "Lilly and Company. You're not in public relations. I know what you are."

I said, "Look, lady, I run a legitimate business."

And she said, "No. I know what you do and you'd better leave my husband alone." I didn't even know her husband. I must have sent him a card.

My lawyer is a big-brain murder lawyer. He handles me on the side as a friend. When I went into business, he told me what I could and couldn't do. That's why a cop can't pull any shit on me. I quote the law word for word. I've learned it chapter and verse. Every article.

When I go to a hotel to solicit business, a detective may stop me. He'll come up and say, "What are you doing here?"

I say, "Number one, I want your police badge," and then I take all the information down. I give the guy the feeling that he's going to get in big trouble by messing with me and that I'm no common street girl like he's trying to imply.

Inside the hotel, if I start talking to a guy who turns out to be a cop, I can never be charged with soliciting. My lawyer tells me that you can't be charged unless you mention money. I never mention money. Only the penthouse and the beautiful young ladies.

I always check a man who calls on the phone. If he calls and says he's a friend of Mr. Jones, I get Mr. Jones on the other line. I find out what business he's in, not only from him, but from Mr. Jones. I check the business, and when he comes up, get his business card before he can come to the apartment. Detectives are not that thorough. But if a man calls and says, "I'm a friend of Tom Jones," I don't just take him because he knows Tom. Maybe Tom just met him in a bar and he said, "Hey, buddy, I want to get laid." Tom gives him this number and he's a cop. I must check the business. If I'm in doubt, I don't. I'd rather lose a few people than take a chance on losing all my business.

Besides, I can tell if a cop's calling. I have a sixth sense. He starts to talk and I feel something wrong. I talk to him for a minute, ignore my feeling and check him out. Every time, he hasn't checked out. Only when you get careless can you get hurt. When you get lazy and everything's good, you say, "I know Tom Jones. He's an old friend." You take the man and get in trouble. There's no way on earth you can get busted if you're careful.

There can be ten detectives sitting outside my door, and they can't do a thing. First I want to see their I.D.—with the chain-bolt still on the door. Second, I want the search warrant. Then I call my lawyer before I let them in. If they don't have a search warrant, I wait for them to break down the door and then I sue.

I also suggest that I could cause a little trouble. Some of my Government friends could get them fired. A month ago, a detective sat in the lobby downstairs for about two weeks. Then he left. He must have gotten tired of watching me pass—young and dressed conservatively square—knowing that I couldn't be a madam!

One of my girls got picked up by a cop who entrapped her. He approached her on the corner and named a price. It would have been thrown out of court. But now the cop wants a constant payment. I went straight down to court, and in the meantime I found out his captain's name. Then I hit the cop with the situation and bailed the girl out. I said, "I'd like to see your captain, Mr. So and So." He wonders how I know his captain, because he's a captain on the Vice Squad and nobody knows his name. So the cop got scared. If I'd wanted to be larcenous, I could have taken a pay-off from him. But I might get killed that way. It's blackmail.

The Johns that come to a madam are different from the Johns that frequent a high-class call girl. The madam is a mama. These Johns need to be nursed and nurtured. They tell me their problems. If I'm nice and sweet and understanding, they like me. They come back and spend more money. It's not that I'm more intelligent than other madams, but I've seen men react to harsh treatment, and I do know what not to do.

Men always want me, because they want what they can't have. A madam who goes with the men is stupid. One way to get a John coming back is to make him keep wanting you. If I went with him once, forget it. The challenge would be over. As long as they know they can't have me, they keep coming back.

I could make a fortune if I went with men. I've been offered two and three hundred dollars just to let a man go down on me. But I'd only get this money once, I'd spoil my whole image and the guy might not come back. Besides, I'm a virgin.

Men want to adopt me. If anyone ever gives me trouble, I should call them. Since I come across innocent and naive, they feel needed. I let men underestimate me, until they try to pull something on me. I'm generally protected, because a John needs to come to me, not just for sex, but for the attention and to be made to feel important. That's the whole psychology of a madam's success. First build up the John.

I do not let men push me. I have one guy who sticks me with checks—or sometimes credit. It's like pulling teeth to get money out of him. I call and he says, "I'll bring it over next week." But he does spend a lot of money, and, by making him feel he's done something wrong, I make him come more often and spend more money. I don't yell and scream at him. I just make him feel guilty. That works to my benefit. He'll come back out of guilt.

A madam must treat the girls kindly too. I don't threaten them. Girls laugh at threats you don't follow up. They know I couldn't kill a cockroach. If I'm really going to do something, I don't talk about it. I never let them know what I'm thinking. I make them afraid to find out!

I don't treat the girls like shit. I respect them. I project an attitude: "I'm really a great person and you need me. The worst thing in the whole world would happen if I didn't like you." Of course, if I don't like them, there's no business.

There are three kinds of girls. The professional I don't like to deal with at all. She's got no feeling for the man. She's hard and she'd stab me in the back if she got a chance. Professionals have been around for a long time. When you're in the life, you have a decision to make: Will I just look out for myself or will I look at life as a human being and consider other people. You start out treating people like humans and they stab you in the back. This happens over and over again. You become hard and start stabbing other girls. A vicious chain starts and pretty soon you don't care about anybody.

The professional girl tries to treat the client well, but the guy has a feeling about her. He knows she's pretending. These girls become incapable of love and caring. They want to hurt other people and use them. They do this to the man and they do this to the madam. So I'd just as soon stay away from the professional.

My second choice is the square girl. I don't encourage girls to go into this life. But I might be in a restaurant with a friend, and a girl will come up to him and say she needs money. He'll look at me. If I feel she's ripe, I'll say: "I could get you money, but I don't encourage you to do this. If you think you can hack it, I'll get you some business. You can work for me."

When a sixteen-year-old comes and asks you for work, it makes you think. Last week, a girl came in and I said, "Go home to your mother. You shouldn't be in this at sixteen. You should be in school." But she wanted it. She'd been working on the street. I don't usually take street girls, but she was new and I knew I could make a fortune on her. If she didn't get business from me, she'd get it from someone else. So I took her.

Once I decide to work with a square girl, I take her number and give her my card. I don't instruct her, because this work comes naturally. I do tell her that she must do everything I say. If I send her out on a dinner date, I know she's going to give the man her number and see him on her own. If I find her passing her number in my house, I'll throw her out and never see her again. That's like slapping me in the face.

I don't like my guys rushed. I don't like my girls coming on like whores. Anybody can be a lady—no matter what they do. A guy doesn't like to feel he's paying for it, even if he knows he is. My girls must dress conservative and do everything the man wants. They must not rush him; they talk a bit first. When they're done, they don't just jump up and walk out. They talk to him afterward. My girls have a cultivated appearance and style.

The square girl wants the madam to like her, so she's not going to cheat. I don't fear that she'll walk off with my files. The professional doesn't care about me. She'll give her number out if she gets a chance. The square girl is damned and determined to impress me. She wants more business. She doesn't know how to trick me yet.

My first choice is still the gay girl. Besides being the best prostitutes, it might work out that I can find a special personal relationship with a gay. It doesn't make me jealous that she goes with men. I could too. I just don't want to. If a working girl becomes my friend, I'll throw more business her way. I look out for the girls who look out for me. If I love a girl, I do feel a bit sad that she has to work.

BUSINESS WOMEN IN A WORLD OF PLEASURE

A MADAM'S BOOK

CHAPTER THREE

BUSINESS WOMEN IN A
WORLD OF PLEASURE

A Madam's Book

Note: Often a madam keeps a book of photographs of "My Girls."
She presents this book to her customers and they can pick a girl.

KAREN

KAREN: There are other ways I could get the money I need. I made as much money modeling as I do now. But I'd stand for hours and hours. Here I can make fifty dollars an hour and I'm lying down the whole time.

I learned something about men when I started this work. I used to think a man was over a woman, that she should give him everything. I always let my boyfriend boss me around. I'd work three jobs and give him all my money. Then he'd complain that I didn't have any new clothes. I got sick and used to cry and have fits.

Today I called him up and said, "Hey, that new furniture I'm going to buy—it's gonna be mine." He asked how come I was being so pushy. But last week, he'd said that the reason he despised me was because I was a dog—I let him step all over me.

Now we're equal. I realized that today. I've come to feel equal with men who are my customers. Sure, they pay me. But I perform a service. So it's tit for tat. You're on a very equivalent basis with the men who buy you.

NELL

NELL: I like a man who considers you as a person and who is kind to you as an individual. Men can treat you like a sexual object. Like you're just nobody. They come to get a thrill and that's it. You have no personality. They don't talk to you and they handle you roughly. I like someone who's gentle and considerate.

I'm helping out a boyfriend, otherwise I'd still be a hairdresser. In hairdressing, you express yourself in the design of the hair. In this business, you can express yourself by making each man an individual. I have as many as fifteen men a day and make between five hundred and a thousand dollars a week.

You learn responsibility as a prostitute. I've learned how to grow up. I've gotten an education in people, because customers come from all over the world. If you listen to these people, you can broaden your horizons.

$\mathcal{LISA}$

LISA: In Los Angeles, I used to have a multimillionaire sugar daddy. He took care of me, gave me two thousand dollars a week, and only saw me once a week. If I didn't feel like doing anything with him, I'd call one of my friends and give her fifty dollars to go to bed with him. I liked that life. I'd do some things on the side, but never for less than three hundred dollars.

My mistake was a boyfriend. Even though he had his own apartment, he used to sleep with me every night. One day, my sugar daddy called and said, "I'll be over in a half an hour." He came in ten minutes and I couldn't get my boyfriend out fast enough. My sugar daddy never said anything to me, but I never saw him again. That hurt.

Me as a person, I really dig sex. Some customers, I have a climax with. When this happens, I feel like I don't need a boyfriend. A boyfriend bugs you for money and spends so much time with you. You can't make money, because you can't concentrate on your work. Let me have my sexual fun with tricks and forget the boyfriends.

$\mathcal{A}\mathcal{M}\mathcal{A}\mathcal{N}\mathcal{D}\mathcal{A}$

AMANDA: I'm in this business for a goal. I want to get some money together and go home to New Hampshire to marry my boyfriend. This is a short-term proposition.

I tell a girl not to start in the business. It's a disease, because you can get money so easily. But you never gain. When you're forty, you don't have anything to show for your work. You might have a groovy apartment and very groovy clothes. But that's not worth the hassle. You make a lot of money, but it goes as it comes. Easy.

Females in this life are more into sex than other people. They do not have common sex. For money, you do different things. Men spank me; I beat them up and yell at them.

At first I was afraid to have a masochist John. I learned by being a slave to another girl. The John was being a slave too. My girlfriend told me to answer, "Yes master," "No master," and do whatever she said.

"You're going to be my slave." That's exactly what she told me. "Kiss my feet." The guy was jerking himself off.

Now I enjoy the masochists. It lets out my frustrations. You call the John nasty names, you tell him to lick the toilet, and pee on him. I couldn't handle that before.

I walk into a room and a man just tells me what he wants. I go and tie him up. He likes the crack of the whip. That gets him off. The guys who ask for it are nuts, but whipping is better than fucking all the time. I like fucking, but not everyone. I don't want to get too stretched out. The masochists help preserve me.

I think every person is a bit masochistic. I get myself into situations that I know will harm me and I let them go by. Being a call girl is destructive to my body. The hours are rough. Men ball you constantly. I am somewhat masochistic myself.

I don't like the girls in the business. In plain English, they're cunts. They're very mean, hard, crude, and out for themselves and their pimps. They see how they can take advantage of you and slit your throat.

Call girls are the biggest tricks in town. They're out making money all day long and then they pay their guy—a pimp. Pimps are the biggest whores. They're selling their bodies to their girls. And they sell their minds, which are very small. If I can outfool most of the pimps I've met, they can't have very big brains.

Uusually I meet pimps and go out with them to party and ball. They know I'm not for grabs. If I went for their lines—"I'm in love with you, et cetera"—forget about it. They get girls by bullshit and by their supposedly great sex. They are good at sex, because that's their business. And that's the only reason I go out with them. The Johns don't satisfy me. Hustlers do. Pimps. Mafiosa types. People who blow coke can keep it up for a long time. Alcohol makes it go down. Pimps blow coke and Johns drink. That's the heart of the problem.

I've accomplished something since I've been a prostitute. I feel better. I don't have to depend on anybody. I've got confidence about being female. For someone to pay a hundred dollars to me—I don't think I'm an ugly little thing. When a John picks me out of a room of ten girls, it's a compliment.

Being in the business has improved my sex life. Anyone who says no is stupid. I'm hot-blooded and my life fulfills me. Having attention from men is marvelous. Besides, in New York, there's nothing to do but screw. I turn into a different person in the country. When I go home to New England, I don't screw for a month. Last time, I lived with three boys that really wanted me. I didn't touch them. It was good knowing I couldn't be bought with money. I could hold my head high.

I certainly wouldn't want prostitution legalized. There'd be too many girls in the business. And I love to outsmart the cops. The danger makes this life exciting and fun.

[NOTE: Amanda went home and married her boyfriend six months after this interview.]

BETSY: The moment I get my bills paid, forget the Johns. If I'd known any other way to get out of debt, I wouldn't have gone into the business.

I'd known businessmen who used girls for a night. I met them in my regular daytime job. We'd have a ceremonial dinner and I'd meet a few girls who were there for men. They were beautiful-looking girls who intrigued me. I couldn't understand why they did what they did. Men who were paying them would talk about them as hookers—in a degrading way. Never did I dream I'd get the same talk and the same treatment.

When I got in financial trouble, I called one of these girls to ask for help. She sent me up to a madam's party. I felt like meat put on exhibition. I was there for an hour and ran out. Later on, I got my guts together, because things were getting desperate. I didn't have money for food. I needed money not today, but yesterday. I went back to the madam's to start to work.

You've got to have guts to go into the life from a middle-class background. If you've been raised religiously, the business takes a lot out of you. You have to forget everything you've been told.

The only way to go through the first night is not to think about it. You can't afford to analyze. I couldn't say, "This guy's paying me and it's not good." I couldn't think, "My God, I've been with three guys in one night. How could I do it?" I started counting the money and forgot the guilt. I forgot the shame. I remembered that now I could pay the gas bill and have a phone.

I was very depressed for a few days. In order not to go nuts, I set myself a goal. I'd seen my mother nearly starving. I owed a mortgage on the house and I'd tried every way legally to get money. I was doing this for a cause . . . a good cause. After a few days, I got hardened. A doctor sees a patient dying, and the first time he's shocked and can't bear it. After he sees a few people die, he gets used to it. I feel the same way about the business.

I have to go out two or three times a week—socially—to keep my mind straight. I go to a movie, dinner, and dancing. Most men, if· they're with a nice-looking girl, try to go to bed with her, unless the man is very much in love with his girlfriend or wife—which happens very rarely in this century, unfortunately. If a man thinks he can make me, he'll try. My friends don't know I'm to get for any price. So, if a man fails to make me, we had a beautiful evening and he goes home.

I do not enjoy getting paid for sex. I'm liked enough by regular, average men not to worry about being attractive. If I were a dumpy-looking housewife, I might get a kick out of it. My kind of love-making is too good for money. Men can't tell I don't like it. I'm nice and pleasant. I make jokes. Seeing that the guy is paying, I make sure he gets a decent job.

I don't think there's anything I don't know how to do sexually. Number one, I like sex. Of course, there's no comparison between a customer and someone you love. I do have a problem. Sometimes I come with a man who's a customer. I shouldn't. I'm not supposed to, but I cannot control myself. We all have animal in us. If it happens that a guy is doing something in the right spot, you can't help but come. That doesn't mean you enjoy it mentally or spiritually. It's just physical. After the excitement is over, you look at the man and say, "I was with *that thing*!" You're glad to get rid of him.

Most girls like the life because they make easy money. You get used to a certain standard of living. If you quit working, you miss the money, so you go back to work.

If you're a weirdo and like group stuff and strange sex, then prostitution is a pleasant way to satisfy yourself and make some money. Beautiful. But I can't get serious in group sex. If there's a mirror and I can watch other couples, I laugh my head off. It looks like a Mickey Mouse cartoon.

If you're a nymphomaniac, then you might enjoy being a prostitute. Otherwise, it's business. I get satisfaction out of seeing my bills paid. Period. I'm very grateful to the John, because he's helping to pay my bills. But I don't feel anything beyond gratitude. If he didn't pay me, I wouldn't go with the guy. Who needs it? I've got a boyfriend for all my sexual needs. I'll do it as a business, as a profession, because it is a means to an end.

$\mathcal{S}ANDY$

SANDY: I come up to the madam's when my phone's not busy and she has something going on. Mostly I work on my own business—taking care of my clients and sending them to other girls. But I'll work anyplace—in bars and on the street, 'cause I have a guy—a pimp—and I love him very much, so I work hard for *him*.

Men always ask me the same question. Here they are paying me to satisfy them and they're constantly worried about satisfying me: "Did I make you happy?" "Can you reach a climax?"

Money, not satisfaction, is the drawing factor in this life. Many girls that hate the life put on such an act they should be in the movies. They hate every guy that walks in the door, but they do it for the money. I'm not like that. I'm more the social worker type. I've even lost some customers by talking to them.

I had one guy who came to see me once a week and he'd talk about his wife. "Why can't I make my wife happy? What am I doing wrong?" I would talk to him and teach him things, until one night he came to me kind of drunk. I'd never seen him drunk before. He was very upset. He said, "I tried all of this on my wife and now I'm going to tell you the truth. One night about a year ago, I walked into my house early and I caught my wife in bed with my next door neighbor and he was sucking her pussy and she was just loving it. Ever since then I haven't been able to get excited with her." He's impotent. Then he said, "I have no problem with you or with other girls. But with my wife, I can't, because I keep thinking about that day. I want something different. I'm tired of seeing girls."

He's really drunk, right? So I said, "Well, would you like to see a guy?" I knew for a fact he didn't have any homosexual tendencies and that he wouldn't be able to do anything with a guy. But I asked him and he said, "Well, maybe." Like he's willing to try anything.

So I called a guy over and we got all the way up to the point of the actual act and the man all of a sudden snapped out of it, got dressed and went home. I never saw him again. He did call me about a month later and told me that he'd gone home that night and had beautiful sex with his wife and he'd never had another problem again. He needed a sexual shock of some kind. He said, "You might be sorry, because I'm not going to see you ever again." I was happy for him. I can afford to lose a trick.

Prostitution is the oldest profession in the world and it will always be. I don't care how many laws are against it or how strictly those laws are enforced. It's always going to be here. I think it should be legal. The government's losing a lot of money in taxes. At any rate, it's the only way I can keep my guy living in style!

BUSINESS WOMEN IN A WORLD OF PLEASURE

PAMELA

CHAPTER THREE

BUSINESS WOMEN IN A
WORLD OF PLEASURE

℘𝒜ℳℰℒ𝒜
a Madam

NOTE: Pamela ran a high-class house on the East Side of
Manhattan. She considered herself an excellent
businesswoman, although she constantly regretted being
in an illegitimate business. She complained that her father,
a guard in a large New England town—had given her
insufficient direction as a young woman.

During the time I spent at her house, she grossed about
three thousand dollars a week, after splitting fifty-fifty with
her girls. Her expenses were high—the rental on her
penthouse apartment, liquor, sheets and the various

accoutrements of the trade, pay-offs to the personnel in her building, cab drivers, and the omnipresent police. She cleared between fifty and fifty-five per cent of her gross.

Pamela did save her money. One day, on the way to a bank to re-cash a client's check that had bounced, we stopped at her safe-deposit box, which she further crammed with hundred-dollar bills. I sat one afternoon while she signed up with a mutual-fund salesman. She maneuvered constantly to sell stock in a corporation that would buy a brownstone and provide more room for business. Through clientele from the art world, she dealt as a broker in rare coins and paintings. Stockbrokers, who regularly frequented her house, gave her tips and she invested.

Pamela was frequently frenetic, but all of her activities were directed toward an end—to build her own business and find new avenues for financial development. Pamela was not a clothes horse. Her real desire was for self-improvement. As a child, she had studied the piano and one day she got a whim to start lessons again. When Pamela moved, she moved quickly. We immediately went to Yamaha, decided which piano was most suited to her décor, and bought it. Pamela plunked down cash and then offered the overwhelmed salesman some amil-nitrate—whispering that it would keep "it" up. Although the salesman could not accept Pamela's invitation to join us for lunch at the Russian Tea Room, she did offer him a choice of swaps, swingers, and sexy singles.

Pamela had grown up in New England and had been cramped by the cold winters and the cool tempers of her family and friends. When she was seventeen, she left town to work.

PAMELA: The first time I left home, I went by Greyhound Bus. I wanted a warm climate and chose Florida. I got a job in a stock-broker's office—my first and last job working for someone else.

I was often amused. It seemed like every girl in that office was secretary to the boss and received one-hundred-fifty-dollar dresses daily. A beautiful exmodel—about twenty-six and older and wiser than me—decided that the best place to meet rich guys was in a brokerage firm. That's all she took the job for. She received a forty-thousand-dollar home from one customer. Every girl in the office was angling to meet rich men. I finally got a guy to pay my eighty-dollar rent and buy me trinkets and gifts. Nothing. But I wasn't wise and hip to how to get from men in those days. I was a young, nice innocent girl.

The stockbroker—wanting to clinch deals for his own purposes—persuaded me that I shouldn't give sex away for nothing. "If you love sex so much" (and I did), "do it for money." He said he'd take me on his yacht for weekends; I'd meet famous people. All the firm's accounts went on the yacht. I started being included in parties to the Keys. This was my first venture in taking money for sex.

I had a pleasant weekend with about twenty people on board. If there were other call girls, I didn't know. I had the front as the worker. "This is my secretary," the broker would say—pretending I was going to be a freebie. It's more pleasant for a man when he doesn't have to take money out of his own pocket. Even if he knows the girl is a professional, it's better for him mentally.

The broker would tell me which account he wanted me to con-centrate on: "This guy's important. Play up to him." I'd usually see just one man over the weekend, but, if there was a girl shortage, I might take on another. I never transacted business for the broker. I just went to bed. But on the following Monday, when we went back to the office, I'm sure there was a lot more profit going into the broker's pocket. He was a smooth operator and now he's the head of a big company in Florida. I think I was responsible—just a little— for his success.

Then I met a big union man in Miami and he persuaded me to come up to New York. "There's a great opportunity for a girl like you who likes sex and money." When I got to New York, he introduced me to a girl who had her own two-bedroom apartment and was doing a thousand a week. That's nothing to me now, but in those days it seemed grand.

This girl gave me her "leftovers" and introduced me to five madams. I never sat at a madam's house—like it's properly done— changing and rotating girls every two weeks. The madams would just refer men to my home and I'd deliver their cut.

In three months, I made up my mind: I'm going to hate men if I keep this up. I can't work any more. If you see a lot of men every day, you meet some bastards who say, "Show me your wares," "Undress," "Show me the merchandise I'm buying." Some men can be very rude. Those damn cloak-and-suiters are the rudest people in the world compared to the beautiful Wall Streeter or the advertising men. Those men I love—I love the way they sit down and talk about the millions at once; they get you spellbound.

I decided to become a madam. I did it because I love the men— I eliminate the crude guys and keep the beautiful ones. The money's good. I am a good businesswoman and running a house allows me to express my talents.

I had learned one lesson: make money quick if possible. In the next ten years at the most. Then get out. My first book of clients came from a seventy-year-old madam. Balding, and in the business still. Many, many apartment houses she owned, but she just didn't know anything to do but madam. Lonely, lonely. The last I remember her, she had a Bible in her hands—she went completely religious.

I have deep religious feelings beneath me. I still feel that marriage is a once in a lifetime thing. The Catholic way of thinking. I've had many proposals of marriage, but I didn't want them, because I must love the man. That's being a woman. I cannot marry a man just for security—a seventy-five-thousand-dollar home. I've turned it down. Swimming pools, maids, trips to Europe once a year. I don't want it.

Now I've consoled myself with an older man. I don't want him for his money, even though he's worth five million. I don't want him for marriage. I need him for advice. Business advice.

Everyone has a goal in life. I've been a kept woman, I've been a call girl, I've owned businesses, and I've been a madam. The normal goal for a woman is to be a wife, but a woman's fulfillment is children—being a mother. I've had the minks. They don't mean anything any more. I want a child.

If I had a child, I think I could possibly do a quarter of a million a year. Now I do about a hundred fifty thousand. I'd do more than madam. I'd get some new business. A man the other day gave me a new idea: installing time- and labor-saving incinerators in buildings. In Washington, D.C., only the Statler Hilton has them. New York is wide open. If I devoted two hours a day to this, I could sell forty a day with a two-hundred-dollar commission per unit.

I'm in business for money. Madaming is the perfect place to meet presidents of large corporations who give me stock tips. Who gets the first news on new offers—me—sitting in my house of joy. I get a financial education which leads to money, and I like the men.

A Madam's Work

PAMELA: On a typical hard-working day, I make outgoing calls from ten to two. "Hi. How are you?" And then I wait for the callbacks. If I make twenty calls a day, twenty men will come the following week, so it pays.

I keep men's numbers in an address book, without which I'd be absolutely lost. If I go to Europe for a couple of months, how could I remember every name and number? If my phone is disconnected during a raid, I can't count on having the same number myself. So

I must keep careful track of the men myself. I pay attention to trade.

I get business cards and personal information from the customer. He's hesitant to give this information to a call girl. You do have men who think they can get a girl for less if they don't go through the madam. Probably fifty thousand call girls work within a fifty-block radius between 86th Street and 34th Street on the East Side. One apartment building at 77th and York has twenty girls, I know. But when a man wants a girl, he wants her on a moment's notice. I have trouble reaching ten out of forty girls on my list, so it's not likely that a John will find a girl quick and easy. A madam can. That's why a John comes to me.

A sensible man also knows he's safer in a house. I send the girls to the doctor once every two weeks; no new girl can come in without a certificate of clean, good health.

I work in other cities like Los Angeles and Boston on an exchange basis. A customer will come here and say, "What shall I do in Boston?" I use a code and give them a card. They can't get into the Boston house without those credentials.

I know a madam in Boston who has customers that frequently stop over in New York. She will give them my name and number; they come to me when they're here. In addition to exchanging clients, we exchange girls. She has customers who come once a week, so New York girls go to Boston for a week, have a guarantee of five hundred dollars, and get rent and food free. I need a fresh supply of girls for my men, too.

Every two or three weeks, I have to get that address book out and put in an increase of new men's names that come by recommendation. Calling is my main concern to keep the business going. Competition is keen in New York, so I must constantly let men know that I have a variety of girls: "Something new came in this week. Something fantastic." "I have an Oriental specialty."

I might call a man or send him a Christmas card, but he doesn't need my services any more. He's still useful to me, because he sends other men. Members of his firm may need my services. Some old customer may say, "I'm happily married now." But that doesn't mean anything. Happily married or not, he's still permissive!

I have a rich boy who inherited three million. He was rich at twenty-one, and he's richer now because he bought a seat on the Exchange and is part of a firm, too. He just got married. The night before the wedding, he came up here with his little suitcase. A few days later, he's back from the Raquet Club. His wife's a high-society broad, so I was shocked. Then he called a third time: "I'm out walking the dog. Can you sneak one in now? It will have to be quick."

I said, "My God, I thought you were training your wife. When do you have time?" He's certainly not training her very well.

The best men say, then and there, when I call, "Oh, great. I'll be up at four o'clock." I might be busier that very day, because I've called.

A girl comes in to sit around one or two. She's booked in a house for a certain number of weeks. My girls are all screened. None of them can be dope fiends, and if a girl shows the slightest inclination of being drunk, or acts like an idiot, I just throw her out. I don't want her. I don't want trouble.

The only way I can get into trouble is by being greedy, trying to take every girl I meet and add her to my list. A girl must have good references, which I check and doublecheck. A girl could know a policeman or a Vice-Squad man, who'd tell her a name to use. So I can't be stupid enough to take someone by their own recommendation. That's the way to get into trouble. Plain out and out greed.

On a bad day in my house, a girl may make only fifty dollars. If a different girl were booked every week, business might be better. But the same girls usually stay for three or four weeks. The customers have seen her; maybe she's not that different or that pretty. For some reason, she's not making money. Men will say: "That's not my type." "I want a blonde." "I want more bust." "She's not tall enough." The girl has got to learn to take the bad with the good. I will not make up for a bad day by paying the girl money she does not earn. But I will try to throw the girl more business on another day. Of course, you can't force a girl on a man, and if she's really bad, I just throw her out of my house and dismiss her from my mind.

Once I lost my temper, which does not pay. I said, "Listen you tramp, get out of my house. You raid my kitchen. You use my negligees and sit around the house. You just got rid of a pimp and you attempted suicide. You're a plain out and out tramp. Get out." If I've given that girl my private number, she can give it to the Vice Squad or a cop. Then I'm cooked. In this town, there is too much jealousy. One girl informs on another. That's why I have a fixation about never giving my private number out. My private phone is for my social life, which I try to keep separate from business. Sometimes friends knock at the door, or ring the bell—people who know me socially. "Oh, we were just passing by." Ringing the bell with four customers here! No dice.

My business phone is a trunk line and calls come through only at the answering service. I use the answering service's number. My own, private number is connected on a separate line to the answering service's board. That could, unfortunately, get tapped very easily.

But I take care of the answering-service girls. I have to take care of everyone that's important to me. Answering-service girls get dresses earned from the cloak-and-suiters. When I started getting busy, I never talked to the doormen, but I handed out ten-dollar bills. "Take care. Make sure that everybody has a taxi." I never work in a building without clearing it with the superintendent.

Three or four girls sit in in the evening. The men come in groups, because it gives them courage. If a man gets enthused, he can have a vast variety at my house. Often two men and two girls like to get in bed together; then they turn around and exchange. It's per-girl fees—whatever happens.

From four to seven, I'm very busy with the commuters who go to Connecticut every night. I can have six calls within the house at that time. Some men call the day before. But usually they say, "I'll be up in an hour," or "We're going out to dinner, but we'll come up later."

After dinner, they want it immediately. If the man is a visiting fireman, in from out of town, the girl can go to his hotel. But I'd rather have them come up here. Some girls go out on calls at the end of the night—girls I know better than to send on outs. I don't hear from them that night, and the next day, when I call for my money, they say, "I haven't got that much on me." They've gone shopping with my share.

You learn to screen girls, to know which girls are reliable for outs, and which ones you'd better keep in. That's part of training the girls. You also have to teach them how to collect money. In the madam's house, they're never allowed to discuss or touch money. All negotiations are handled by me. But the girls must collect up front on outs, otherwise they may be shortchanged. I will be too.

I get a lot of business from cab drivers. They're hustlers all right. One will call, "I've heard about you . . ." If you get ten cab drivers working until five in the morning, you can build up a Rolodex file of four thousand names—a fantastic following, even if you have to give a big cut to the driver. You only give him the cut the first time. From then on, the client's yours, and what do you care?

Men go to a nightclub where they see pretty girls, but they can't get at them. So cab drivers hang around those clubs, pick up the men when they're hot and bring them over to me. Usually the man is more happy in a house than he is in a bar—just hoping for a girl. So he'll come back again and again.

My social friends recommend men to me. An old Irish drinking buddy who I go out with—he's never used my business—he referred a big Wall Street investment firm. Now this Wall Street guy calls to say that they're having a banking convention at the New York Hilton and he needs four girls. I figured I'd better have eight available. Actually many more were needed that evening.

I went over to the hotel with the girls—to introduce them and collect the money. It was a big amount of money and the first time I was doing business with this firm. A man might try to take advantage of a girl, see her more times than he's allowed for the amount of money he's paid. If I don't go, the girls would have to collect money up front, which is not very dignified. Also, if the girls went up there alone, they might leave when they felt like it. For a hundred dollars, you have to give a man something. A girl must stay with him awhile.

I want diplomacy and a happy customer—one that will return. Men like to talk to me afterward: "I must have her again." "This one is terrific; she's out of sight." They enumerate parts of the anatomy they liked and talk about being happy and fulfilled. They need someone to listen, which is a madam's role.

There's another advantage to going. When you've set up your business, you can visit in other hospitality rooms. I got one man to take me around. He'd say, "Hi, meet a friend of mine." I'd give them a card. "She's in Public Relations." [Pubic, I say]. "You can use her services. I think you can use each other's services." He was tactful about it all. Ten more people I met that night through one contact. That's five hundred more dollars worth of business right then. I could hardly handle half of it.

Of course, some people said, "I've got a girl tonight—a square." Or, "I've got to go home tonight." But they'll call. They will definitely use my services in the future.

I frequently do stag parties for auxiliaries, American Legions, and private men's clubs. The number-one request is for a show. Each girl gets a hundred dollars for making love to the other.

Sometimes as many as four or five hundred men attend. The two girls get in the middle of the floor and go at it. I get one real lesbian—I've got to get the real McCoy, because the men can tell a fake. But men don't want two lesbians. After the show, they're going to go with one of the girls. The aggressive one—maybe they shrug her off. But the other girl sometimes handles thirty men in an evening.

A representative of the club has to come to my house, pay up front, and pick up the girls. I set an amount for the show, the length of time the girls will stay, and the number of men each girl can handle. I get a guarantee, which I collect beforehand. It's not safe for a girl to collect money at the club. Someone will roll her. Nasty things like that have happened. The girl puts her pocketbook somewhere; all the money gets stolen. One girl might even steal from another. It's the madam who loses then, because I always guarantee the girl her share of the money. I still go fifty-fifty. My cut.

Besides men's clubs, a fellow could be getting married. I suggest a stag party with bathtubs full of champagne. Once I even serviced gangsters, but I didn't know what they were into. There was a card game going on. The man I knew wasn't in the rackets, but he was surrounded by shady characters. I brought five girls up there—two for the show and three for work.

Many men want me. I tell them no. They can't afford me. That chases them away, because they're cheap. Or they want more for their money. Why should I spend time with them if I can madam? I can get on the phone and make a hundred more quickly. If I worked in addition to being a madam, I could make five thousand a week easily. Without working I can do three thousand in five days. That's enough. I always take my weekends off.

One madam I know is forty-five and still in the business. She does about two thousand a week—working seven days a week and fucking every second fifty who comes in. Her feelings get hurt if a John prefers another girl. She throws out both the John and the girl. "I'm much better than those young things."

One weekend, this madam left town, locked the house, and forgot she had one girl living with her. Now this girl had no money in her pocket, one coat, and a dress on her. The girl called her lover and they robbed the madam of sixty-thousand-dollars' worth of minks, sables, and anything they could put their hands on. They even took her address book, which they came to sell to me.

Now here's this madam at forty-five—with a facelift and big boobs. She treats her girls cruelly: "You fucking cockroach. You cunt." I've had girls escape from her house at four in the morning and come to me. I'd never treat my girls that way. Girls want to work for me, because they know one thing: I'm honest and decent and straight.

This way of life is not the easiest way to make money. For a call girl, maybe. She just lays on her back and doesn't use her mind. It's a headache for me.

To be sure, I have advantages. Almost all household items can be gotten by barter. Furniture comes for tricks. A druggist provides all the needed bathroom articles in return for trade. I get eye shadows

in every color of the rainbow, Ramses, douche bags, and mouth washes—the basics of the business. The druggist comes here once a week in return.

But I'm faced with all kinds of problems. A man arrives with no money and no checks. He wants to leave a diamond ring as collateral. He says it's worth a trick. What do you do?

I'm also faced with the possibility that a girl will go through a man's pockets and rob him. I must make sure that the girls are kept honest. This creates mental strain. If you lay on your back for four fifties a day, you clear two hundred. I have to gross four hundred with my fifty-fifty split to make that same money. My work is hard; my money, hard-earned.

An Evening's Entertainment

About nine thirty in the madam's apartment. Three clients are waiting in the living room to be serviced. Only one girl, Chris, is sitting in; two others are expected momentarily. A silent sex film is being screened. The doorbell rings. The madam goes to the foyer off the living room to find four more men outside.

MADAM: [Irritated] *My god. The mirror men. Come to put up the mirror during business hours. Don't you have the common courtesy to call?*

MIRROR MAN: [Insistent] *I did call.*

MADAM: *You did not. I didn't get a message.*

MIRROR MAN: *Well, not today.*

MADAM: *I've got three clients here!*

MIRROR MAN: [Laughing] *You're kidding!*

[The phone rings and the madam goes to answer it in the living room. As they sit watching the stag film, her clients talk.]

CLIENT 1: *I should have brought some food for her dog.* [To Chris, who sits with them] *Send the broads out, will you? I'm not going to mess around with dogs and guys.*

CLIENT 2: [Tittering as he watches the film] *Listen, I know that guy. I recognize him by his balls.*

[Madam retreats from the telephone and addresses Chris.]

MADAM: *Listen. Call this girl back. I can't reach her and she's going to louse up four fifties.*

CLIENT 1: [Aside] *I'll go for fifty!*

[The madam turns to her clients.]

MADAM: [Now the hostess] *If I were a man for six months of the year and a woman for the other six, which way would I do better?*

CLIENT 1: *As a man.*

MADAM: *You're right. Because I've got a man's head ...*

CLIENT 1: *That's why you called the other broad a cunt ...*

MADAM: *...and a woman's wits.*

CLIENT 1: *... because you've got a man's head. Every broad I see, I call a cunt.*

⟦Chris turns from the phone, where she is talking to a girl working outside the house. She calls to the madam.⟧

CHRIS: *Lorna says the place is so crowded that they won't let the girls in the door.*

MADAM: *Oh, marond! Here's a phone number for the John. Call that number. Mama mia. That Lorna causes me trouble.*

CLIENT 2: ⟦Reacting to a display of fellatio on the screen⟧ *That girl has no tonsils!*

CHRIS: ⟦To phone⟧ *Lorna, call this number and ask for Bob Richards.*

MADAM: ⟦To Chris, as the situation becomes more chaotic⟧ *And tell Lorna to confirm what happens.* ⟦She turns to the mirror men⟧ *You guys didn't come here to measure the mirrors!*

MIRROR MAN: *It's hard to keep our eyes on the wall.*

MADAM: *Don't tell me for aesthetic reasons I can't have a mirror on the wall. Tend to business. Here's pen and paper and a measuring stick.* ⟦She turns back to her clients⟧ *Just barging in like this!* ⟦She sings⟧

> *One, two, three.*
> *Don't you see,*
> *This could mean*
> *A raid for me.*

CHRIS: *She had them paged and there was no answer.*

CLIENT 1: *Well, let's go. I don't want a man tonight.*

MADAM: ⟦To clients⟧ *Those guys are unexpected. They're leaving, baby.*

⟦The phone rings and the madam goes again to pick it up. Her clients refocus on the film.⟧

CLIENT I: *Let the movies go on.*
CLIENT 2:   *That girl has cheap panties on, I tell you.*
CLIENT 3:   *They usually don't wear pants in these pictures.*
MADAM: ⟦To mirror men⟧ *And I want one over the princess bed. A circular mirror to match the bed.*
MIRROR MAN: *I'll take care of it in a few days, okay?*
⟦The madam finally reaches her client from a Wall Street firm by phone.⟧
MADAM: *You're presenting a big problem. Maxwell's Plum is so crowded. The girls paged you there and they've come and gone. You cannot bring them up to my pad for another hour. I can send you to their apartment . . . You did it in such a stupid, assinine way, sweetheart. Telling me to get the goddamned fucking cunts down there to Maxwell's Plum. It's just a fucking pickup joint for secretaries.*
⟦The madam instructs her outside client to go to a girl's apartment and hangs up just as the mirror men leave.⟧
MIRROR MEN: ⟦To clients⟧ *Good night and good luck, fellows. And see you soon, Pamela. Remember our payment. Chris looks pretty good.*
MADAM: *We'll see who's here next week.*
⟦Another girl, Yvonne, enters the apartment, and is introduced by the madam.⟧
CLIENT I: *Everyone enjoys his first time here!*
YVONNE: *What's your name?*
CLIENT 2:   *Russ.*
MADAM: ⟦Singing⟧ *No matter how hopeless . . . That can upset the applecart, four guys walking in like that. That's a bold, fucking Jew. You know what he says to me: "We'll take it out in trade . . ."*
CLIENT I: *I'm not a bold, fucking Jew. I'm just a Jew. I want to be a fucking Jew, please!*
MADAM: ⟦Pursuing her own thoughts⟧ *That guy says, "I'll send my son up for measurements." Some son!*

CLIENT 2:	*Well, the son has friends.*
MADAM:	⟦Remembering again to entertain⟧ *You know the difference between the big cat and the little one? The big cat will scratch your eyes out, but little pussy will never hurt you. Hey, what business are you guys in? Toys?*
CLIENT 1:	*Yeah, toys.*
MADAM:	*Who's in charge here?*
CLIENT 1:	*I am, sweetheart.*

⟦Madam starts singing again, "Love, my song is . . ." and Yvonne calls to the dog.⟧

YVONNE:	*Come here, Rex.*
CHRIS:	*You degenerate. Hey, look what I did to my eyelashes. I got them on in little pieces.*
YVONNE:	*Why is only one eye done?*
CHRIS:	*I didn't have time. One eye has lashes an inch long and the other's naked.*
CLIENT 1:	⟦Teasing⟧ *Oh, yeah?*
YVONNE:	*Are you all from New York?*
CLIENT 2:	*Rhode Island.*
CHRIS:	*I've been in Rhode Island once.*
YVONNE:	*I know one person in Rhode Island.*
CLIENT 1:	*Well, now you know four. Another five and you'll know the whole population.*
YVONNE:	*What are you in town for—the toy show?*
CLIENT 1:	*Yeah, but it ended last week.*
CHRIS:	*I want a Barbie doll.*
CLIENT 2:	*If I'd known, I would have brought you one.*
CHRIS:	*I want one that does all those things—moves her arms and legs . . .*
CLIENT 2:	*They do everything now—almost.* ⟦To his cohorts⟧ *Hey, you guys, we should have brought them here!*
CHRIS:	*I like to play with them for real. When I go home, I play with my little sister's cut-out dolls.*
YVONNE:	*Do you still have toy soldiers—that you wind up?*

CLIENT I: *We have a lot of mechanical toys.*

CHRIS: *Listen. I went to the hairdresser's . . .*

CLIENT 2:   ⟦With mock interest⟧ *When?*

CHRIS: *I went to the hairdresser's around the corner and they charge me ten bucks, right? So I get out of there and I look just like I got out of bed.*

CLIENT I: *Do you think it's easy to make you look like you just got out of bed? Anybody can make you look like you just got out of the beauty parlor . . . but . . .*

CLIENT 2:   *Did they know your business?*

CHRIS: ⟦Serious⟧ *I don't think so.*

CLIENT 2:   *I think they did. They were just trying to give you a professional image. And they got the look. If only you'd remember what you do!*

⟦Chris goes over and cuddles next to the man.⟧

CHRIS: *I didn't forget, baby.*

⟦Yvonne is attempting to thread the projector. She's going to screen another film.⟧

CHRIS: *That's not right. You have to stick it in that little hole.*

CLIENT I: *I wish I could . . . but I think we're being charged fifty bucks to watch these films.*

YVONNE: *Want another film?*

CLIENT I: *What are you doing? Asking us?*

CLIENT 2:   *If we wanted one, would you know how to put it on?*

CLIENT 3:   *We weren't really watching the film.*

CLIENT 2:   *It's in the price, whether you want it or not.*

CLIENT I: *I don't believe this. You get some pictures so you know how to do it.*

CLIENT 2:   ⟦Mock serious as Yvonne continues to be frustrated by the projector⟧ *I came up for the movies. What will I do if there isn't a movie?*

YVONNE: *How about dirty books? I went to a card game tonight . . .*

CLIENT 2: 〚Teasing〛 *What did you play?*

YVONNE: 〚Coy〛 *Never mind. I just watch.*

CHRIS: *I went to a crap game once and the guy said, "I bet you five." I thought it was five dollars. Or five hundred. But when he lost, he said, "I'll bring over your five thousand to the office next week."*

CLIENT 1: *Money's only relative . . .*

CHRIS: *There was at least a hundred thousand dollars floating around . . .*

CLIENT 1: *Does money really impress you that much?*

CHRIS: *Well, I've never seen a hundred thousand dollars before . . .*

CLIENT 1: *Does a hundred dollars impress you?*

CHRIS: *No.*

CLIENT 1: *Does three hundred dollars impress you?*

CHRIS: *No.*

CLIENT 1: 〚Laughing〛 *Then give us our money back!*

CHRIS: 〚Defensive〛 *But you see that every day.*

YVONNE: *Who were those guys coming out the door when I came in?*

CLIENT 1: *Oh, they just dropped by for tea . . .*

CLIENT 2: *They were just passing through . . .*

CHRIS: *They said they came to measure the mirrors.*

CLIENT 2: *I've got to go and look at the mirrors. Come on Chris.*

〚Chris gets the point and goes off with Client 2.〛

YVONNE: *How about a film?*

CLIENT 1: *How about a film?*

CLIENT 3: *What about a book?*

CLIENT 1: *We've gone to the movies . . .*

〚The doorbell rings and a third girl enters.〛

YVONNE: *Hail, hail, the gang's all here!*

CLIENT 1: *Why don't you show me the bed now?*

YVONNE: *Let's all go.*

〚The living room empties.〛

The Girls

PAMELA: Getting girls is not difficult. If you're starting as a madam, you have to convince a girl that she can make as much money with you as with the next madam. But after that, you have many more girls than you can find work for.

I meet girls through pimps. Besides movies and an occasional ride in the Cadillac, a pimp's girls have very little entertainment. After twelve, they go to after-hour spots, which are the easiest places in the world to make contacts. To get to an after-hours spot, you take the service elevator in a building. Outside the door stands a guard, who makes sure you're not police. He screens everyone, so you have to know the code, or come with a person known to the guard. Inside are dope, liquor at three dollars a shot, pimps, and their women.

I also go to colored and white hangouts like Small's in Harlem. At three or four in the morning, you mingle in with the pimps. If you spot a girl alone, you go boldly across the room and say, "Do you know and so?" The names of the other big madams in town.

If the girl is with her pimp, you can't talk directly to her, because she'd say, "I have to talk to my man." You can't go directly to the pimp, because this is his girl's night off—and her time to be a lady. To be more subtle, I ease over and say, "Hi, there. Here's my name and number. If you're interested in making at least five hundred a week, let me know, 'cause I could do a lot for you. And if you want to check me out, here's a few other names." I do get results.

A pimp appreciates a madam's efforts. He wishes more people would go out and find his girls. Deep down, he hopes that the madam will send clients to the girl's own apartment, because she'll get their number for herself and forget me and my cut.

Four women might work for one pimp at a time. A girl will refer one of her "wives-in-law" to me. It's just a chain reaction through the pimp's women. A pimp might also come directly to me for work for his women. He has one girl working a bar. She gets fifty for each guy, but she has to give ten to the man in charge of the bar and she can only handle three or four men a night. Another of his girls has a book, but she's too stupid to use it and she doesn't have the guts to call up a strange guy. I call and say, "Hello, John Doe. How are you?" In twenty minutes, he knows me. Then I ask, "Are you busy? Why don't I call you back later today or next week?" Once I've gotten to know a man, it's easy from there on out. This pimp's girl can't or won't handle the phone, so he sends her to me.

Answering services can also be of help. Operators will refer girls to a madam's number. We all use the same service. A girl's number is, of course, confidential business. The operator would never give that out. But she might give the girl a madam's number. The girl follows up by calling me.

If I'm hard up and have a shortage of girls, I can always call a cloak-and-suiter for a cheap girl. The clothing manufacturers call for more entertainment than any other profession. In the cloak-and-suit district, businessmen make a contract with a girl for a set amount at the end of the day. When the week is over, she's not paid per man, but by a set-amount check. She's glad to make a little extra with me.

I tell a girl that she's due at a certain hour and obligated to sit for a specified length of time. Then she gets nigger rich with two or three hundred a day and begins to take me for granted. Instead of showing up at one, she'll come at five in the evening. After a while, I have to call other girls, but before I know it, I've gotten two or three unreliable girls coming in.

I control my girls, not through fear, but by letting them know who's ahead of the game. This is business to me; I know it in and out. I sent one girl on a hundred-dollar date. She reports that when she arrived, the man already had a girl so he didn't need her. Now the other girl says she didn't see the man either. I'm sure that one of them got the guy, so I have to play a trick on both girls, because I haven't got my cut. I send them both out on dates which I claim are a certain price. The real price is double, but I make sure the man does not explain the money involved. To the girls' faces, I'll say, "Don't try to put anything over on me, darlings." And then I let them think they've pulled the wool over my eyes.

When a girl starts out, I'll tell her, "If I find out you've lied, I'll never call you a liar, because the most you can say is no. The most I can say is, 'I can't use you any more.' But why do that? We both need each other. You're thinking you're screwing me and I know I'm six jumps ahead of you. I have the customers. Your services are needed, but you're not the only bitch in the world. For that reason alone, I'll keep you in mind, but if I knew you were dishonest, you'd be the last on the line."

Usually I don't bother to check with each man who's seen one of my girls outside the house. I may not hear from him again for a week or two months. I may not hear from him at all. It slips my mind to ask if he gave the girl any more. He's supposed to tell me. But if a girl proves her honesty by reporting an extra hundred dollars, I give her more business. The dishonest girl loses out in the long run. Honesty pays off.

Fifty percent of my girls I don't have to control at all. The pimp controls them. He pushes his own women. One girl may say, "I'm so sore. I don't know what's wrong with me. I had an Xray." She's holding her stomach—this girl with a pimp and two wives-in-law. But she's always afraid she's going to loose her man. A pimp's girl feels badly if she isn't out working. One girl broke out crying, she was in so much pain. It was pathetic. She couldn't make money, because she was sick. But for him, she had to keep working.

A pimp brought a girl to me and said he'd copped her—which means he's gotten her to join his group. Now he has two girls. But the first girl doesn't want to train the new one. In fact, she doesn't want any part of her. Not because the copped girl's better looking. She's probably plainer without that much to offer. Here she is with one suitcase in her hand when he meets her. He throws her into a hotel at a daily rate. He's doing her a big favor—he doesn't even have to show her a good time. Anything—even his body—is enough to satisfy her. She's so lonely: a gaga idiot, new to the city.

So the pimp brings her to me. I let her go to bed with the cloak-and-suiters first—so she can get some clothes. In the house, I'll give her one of my negligees. I'll take a bigger percentage, because she's green and has to be trained and tutored. I could never use her cold.

I tell her how long to be with a man; how to be polite with him. "Don't be reading a book when he walks in. Talk intelligently." That part cannot be definitely guaranteed! I tell her how to get a man relaxed and untense. Give her an idea: "Jump into the bathtub with him—fill the tub with champagne." "Serve him drinks—would you like a drink, sir." The girl should ask the man about his business, but under no circumstances should she ask for his name or number. Three weeks after she's been in my house, I'll go through her address book when she isn't looking. My own numbers will be there. The girls with pimps are taught to be thieves and to be treacherous. They'll take any number they can get.

Deceiving men sometimes give the girl their name, so they can call a girl back direct. If they sense a girl is new at the game, they bargain for a lower price, or for the same price they can get more time.

The girl is instructed about the time element in my house. Men get a half an hour for fifty dollars and an hour and a half for a hundred. People say I give too much for a hundred. But as far as I'm concerned, the men are the most important.

I sent an amateur out on a twenty-five-dollar affair. She made a romance out of it. For three hours, she stays with the guy, because *she's* lonely. "Oh, he wanted to take me to dinner tomorrow night," she whines. I must remind her that she's due for sitting at my house. If she disappears the next night, I know she's seen him. So she'll be at my house.

There is a reason why every girl's in this business. Some are just plain lonely. Others have pimps. I pity the girl with a pimp. If she doesn't bring the money home, he'll drop her or threaten to drop her. Her security is the home he furnished and all those clothes. If she has to leave, she leaves the apartment and all her clothes for the next girl. She leaves the Cadillac too—all of which was earned by her hard work.

Why does a girl go to a pimp? She needs kindness. Pimps are sweet and flash thousands at the start. They wine and dine a girl. Of course, that's just psychology. He's winning her over, and he'll make ten thousand dollars back on the thousand he blew on her that first two weeks in town. But if the girl comes from Kentucky or the West Virginia hills, or if she's a dumb hillbilly from South Carolina, she'll go for a pimp. For a Southern girl, it's rebellion. They go more for the Negro than the white man. Southern girls do everything their parents taught them never to do.

I got near a pimp one time. I couldn't stand him. Obnoxious. With a gold tooth in front. He took me out when he was wearing one of those two-hundred-fifty-dollar suits. It gave me a big thrill. I was in the mood for jazz and I made him spend money on me. At first he said, "No, you treat me." Pimps are used to being treated by the girls, so I thought I'd make this goddamn Negro pimp treat me. I ordered champagne and spilled it on his suit. He didn't say, "You have to pay for the cleaning bill." He said, "You bitch. Buy me a new suit." He's so used to being the pimp he forgot what role he was playing.

I said, "Send me the cleaning bill, but don't show your face again to me, you black bastard. Go back South where you belong and take a one-way ticket. 'Cause I can't stand the way you overpower white girls with force and fear."

Pimps don't always make the girls. Sometimes girls make pimps. There's a call girl up the street that did that. She made three thousand dollars a week in her prime. But she needed a man of her own, so she found this beautiful twenty-year-old boy and put seventy thousand dollars in his hands for a business. He blew it. Then she bought him a Cadillac, clothed him beautifully, and took away his masculinity. They'd married, but he broke away from her to do something with his own mind and himself. He's making money now—his own. They're back together.

Things have changed for them. He's bringing the money home. He's asked her to quit, but she won't. She's making retirement money—a thousand a week. She's getting up there in years, but she's good for cultivation. She'll cultivate a man who's good for three hundred a week. If she has three of those going, she's all right. But she's one-hundred-percent wrong. Greed, plain utter greed makes her continue as a call girl. He's a man now and she should quit. She's making a fool of the man and a fool of herself. If she loses him this time, she'll turn to liquor for escape and completely destroy herself. This man is no longer a pimp of his own accord. She makes him one.

I don't have any hangup with keeping a young parasitical fuck on the side. I don't want to marry a pimp in disguise. There's a reputable Jewish boy in town here, married a girl that was going to be extradited back to Jamaica. She was a madam, but they found counterfeit money in her house—with a machine. She took the rap. You don't fuck around with a second game if you're a madam. You can't. So she took out nine months and he ran the business for her. Everything is in his name now. He wised her up on how to run her business properly. "Don't you work anymore, honey, I love you too much." She fell for that line of shit and married him.

She's supposed to be great in bed, but that's not going to keep a man who's a greedy, greedy son of a bitch to lower himself to be a pimp. He's a reputable lawyer on the side. My own lawyer didn't even know he was a pimp.

It's very difficult for a call girl to have a social life. Her hours are hectic. The only people who go along with those hours are men who don't work—like pimps. Girls complain that with straight men, they're in bed when the men work. When they're getting up, the men are just going to bed. But why can't they get a bartender? At four o'clock in the morning, he's through and you're through. Or get a musician or an actor? A lot of musicians go with girls because they like dope. Struggling actors are always with girls who feel sorry for them and give them a place to stay.

If you're a worker, the life can give you a social life. I'd hold out for the top guys; I'd be at the Copa once a week. Every night, I'd eat at the Colony. Some girls work for fifty in the afternoon and have a man who keeps them in the evening. Those are smart girls. I don't envy them, but they do well for themselves.

This business is exciting for a certain type of girl. If she's a clothes horse, she's out there dining and dancing every night, showing off her clothes. There can be a lot of glamour and travel with elegant men to exciting places, foreign lands.

Status is important to every girl in the business—the minks, the

Lincoln Continental—those she must have. A girl with a pimp is particularly conscious of the show. He must have a brand new Cadillac every year, two-hundred-dollar suits, and she, sharp clothes and a mink. That is status.

One girl judges another by the way she dresses and drives around. Girls never make less than five hundred a week, whether they work for a madam or on their own. Every girl makes at least twenty-five thousand a year—that's tax free.

I knew one girl who used to be a cocktail waitress. She loved sex. This life for her was a necessity. Instead of being a silly cocktail waitress getting pinches on her behind, she has an orgasm with two or three men a night. This business is good for her and she's good for two thousand a week, because she enjoys every bit of it. She has three bank accounts, three mink coats, and she's in demand.

Generally, it's services for services rendered. Here and there you'll find a good man. But how can a girl—if she sees an average of six men daily—come with every man? It's physically impossible.

All the girls that work for me are at least acceptable. Foreign girls are very popular, especially since American women's liberation! Men love the cute little French accents. A man may complain: "Boy, I got a dog from you last week. When am I going to get a winner?" Maybe he's gotten ten winners, but he only remembers the dog.

I tell him, "Listen, it's like the horses. You get a winner. You get a loser. Here you get winners and losers, too." He'll come back.

Girls get to know each other at my house. That's beneficial to them. In a big city, girls work for a number of madams. They refer each other to different madams. Most girls also have their own business on the side. If a girl's client wants somebody different, she can set him up with a girl she met at my house. But if a girl works at home and wants a repeat performance, she has to have lots on the ball. Men won't come back if she's bad in bed or if they're bored. A cultured woman has a great advantage, because men like to talk to her. But she still has to be a good ball.

Of course, a girl who has her own apartment will take my client's numbers quickly, so I'd rather have out-of-town girls. I'll even let them live in and pay me rent. That's the best way to keep my clients.

Behind my back, one girl says to another, "Without me, the madam's lost. She needs me." But the girl wouldn't talk that bullshit to my face. She wouldn't dare, because she fears me and she has too much respect. Behind my back, it's still, "Without me, what would she do?"

What would I do? There are always girls to be booked. I have local girls and girls from out of town and out of the country. The girls are only here to please men. Most men are satisfied with any reasonably attractive girl.

Of course, more men would rather please than be pleased. They come to a house to please the girl, which is very hard, because she's out to please him. So you have Jean Smith out to please John Doe, who comes to the house to please Jean Smith.

Business

[Jill leads her customer down the hallway to one of the madam's bedrooms.]

JILL:	*My name is Jill. What's yours?*
ENRICO:	*Enrico.*
JILL:	[She can't quite make him out] *Ricky?*
ENRICO:	*Enrico. I don't speak English.*
JILL:	[Cheerful] *You don't speak English. I don't speak any Spanish!*
ENRICO:	*I don't speak nothing.*
JILL:	*But we don't have problems communicating.*
ENRICO:	*No problem.*
JILL:	*We have a universal—our bodies will speak for each other.*
ENRICO:	*I don't understand you.*
JILL:	*No? Let's see. I'll have to show you.*
ENRICO:	*Mmmm?*
JILL:	*I'll show you. Don't be embarrassed.*

[Jill and her client go into the bedroom, and she begins to undress him.]

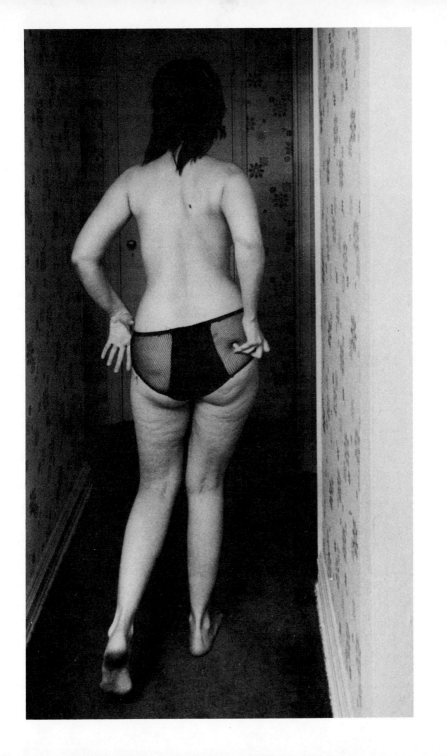

JILL: *Oh, how pretty. These are pretty, sexy underpants.*

ENRICO: *Pretty?*

JILL: *Bright orange.*

ENRICO: [Pointing to the bed] *You get that side.*

JILL: *Hello there, pretty one. I like that!*

ENRICO: *You are too much. I am at this moment disconcerted with you. This is my first time in New York.*

JILL: *I come from Chicago. Give me a kiss. Oh yes. Ah. Yes. Yes, I love to have my breasts kissed. Such a good kiss. See, you don't have to speak English . . . mm . . . ah . . . Oh, suck my pussy. That's good. Oh, this is my day. I really like that.* [He enters her.] *You're such a gentleman. Oh . . . mm . . . mm . . . yes, honey. Yes, I'm going to come for you.* [Gasps] *Oh, yes. That's enough for a minute. Your turn. I came all ready.*

ENRICO: *Was it good?*

JILL: *You kidding me?* [He tries to enter her again.] *Oh, don't touch me there. It's so tender and sensitive now. It can't be touched for a minute. You can't touch it . . .*

ENRICO: *I know this time is very good, yes?*

JILL: *Your turn.*

ENRICO: [Begging] *Please. You.* [He persists in trying to mount her.]

JILL: *I'm too sensitive. Give me you. Oh, let me suck it.*

ENRICO: *You come again?*

JILL: [Pants] *Yes . . . yes.*

ENRICO: *I understand that very well. Nice. Beautiful. You can't have too much.*

JILL: *Wow. Nice . . . nice . . . nice.*

ENRICO: *I tickle.*

JILL: *I'll get a towel.*

[She leaves the room and comes back with a douche bag and towel. She starts to douche.]

ENRICO:	*Before me? You do that before me?*
JILL:	*Well, sometimes people want to see me use it.*
ENRICO:	*Men?*
JILL:	*Yeah.*
ENRICO:	*No! Yes?* ⟦He laughs⟧ *Very wonderful for men.*
JILL:	*Thank you very much. It's been quite a pleasure.*
ENRICO:	*Huh?*
JILL:	*Thank you.*
ENRICO:	*I say thank you. I go to my country after ten days.*
JILL:	*Where? Mexico?*
ENRICO:	*No, Colombia.*
JILL:	*That's such a beautiful country, isn't it?*
ENRICO:	*When do you go to Colombia? Would you like to go? Good people. Good country.*
JILL:	*That's where they make coffee?*
ENRICO:	*Big business in Colombia.*
JILL:	*Really? Think I'd do well there?*
ENRICO:	*Yes. Good in Colombia. You like here?*
JILL:	*I work every day from twelve noon on.*
ENRICO:	*That was so good. I'm going now. I will come back.*
JILL:	*Give me a kiss . . . oh, that was good. Bye.*

⟦ After Enrico leaves, Jill returns to the living room, where Jackie is also sitting in.⟧

JILL:	*God, these men who want to satisfy you. You can't fake once. Twice it's got to be. All I want to do is blow them. It's all I can do to keep their cocks out. And all that panting and gasping is tiring. I hope he doesn't come back.*
JACKIE:	*I went out this afternoon. I saw a guy who always takes about thirty thousand dollars and shows it to me.*
JILL:	*He's just waiting to get robbed.*
JACKIE:	*He shouldn't advertise that he has that much money in his house.*

JILL: *I'm telling you, he wants to get robbed. When I first came to New York, and I was walking the streets for a couple of days because I didn't have a place to work, the first guy I meet walking out of the hotel keeps looking at me. So I says, "Do you want to go out?"*

And he says, "How much?"

So I says, "How much do you want to spend?"

He says, "New York police." So we go up to the room, and he says, "I want you to do something unusual. Tie me to the bathroom door." His wallet's on the bureau and he's paid already. The first day, I didn't take any money. But the second day, I leave while he's still tied to the bathroom door, and take seventy-five dollars from his wallet. The next day, he passes me on the street and I pretend like I don't know him. But he says, "Do you want to go with me?"

So I say, "Yes," but I think the guy's going to do something funny, because I stole his money. So I tie him up again and steal his money again. There're a lot of guys who want to be robbed. They pay you, but they make it so obvious.

JACKIE: *I was going to do so many things today—pick out a pair of shoes, get a couple of outfits from my cloak-and-suit guy. I didn't do a thing.*

JILL: ⟦*Putting on some make-up*⟧ *Oh, I got the wrong color blush-on today. Don't you want to buy it?*

JACKIE: *You're always trying to sell me something you don't want. I got that Yardley today. You put it on and your skin shines. Want to try it?*

JACKIE: *This is shiny.* ⟦*Trying it on*⟧ *It's sparkling.*

⟦Pamela enters the room.⟧

MADAM: *I have big hopes for tonight, so I have four or five glasses out already.*

JILL: *That's bullshit. Because all the guys think their glasses are used. They say, "Give me a clean one." I say, "What do you think this is, a crummy restaurant?"*

MADAM: *No, we're just expecting the army. I'm such a busy, busy bee. I sent Marmelita on an out.*

JACKIE: *I know her.*

MADAM: *She frequents those after-hours spots you frequent until seven or eight in the morning.*

JACKIE: *That's not true. Just because I took you once.*

MADAM: *I know you. I call you at three when you know our day starts at one, and you say, "What is it, eleven?" Calling you at the ungodly hour of three. I do know that it's unheard of to call anyone in your shoes before twelve noon. That's against principles. But four o'clock.*

JACKIE: *I went to bed late.*

MADAM: *Another after-hours spot?*

JACKIE: *I didn't. Anyway, you my mother?*

JILL: *Hey, I'll call Jack and see if he wants someone.*

JACKIE: *Another weirdo! Okay.*

JILL: ⟦Talking to Jack on the phone⟧ *I just called a girlfriend of mine, and she'd like to come over sometime and meet you . . . she's real pretty . . . she likes to do all kinds of things . . . you want to speak to her? She's right here.*

JACKIE: *Hi, Jack . . . Oh, a little bit of everything.*

JILL: ⟦Coaching her⟧ *Tell him you'll piss in his face.*

JACKIE: ⟦To phone⟧ *All right. I'll see you later.*

JILL: *Ask him whether he's going to give you a check or cash. Sometimes he pays by check. They're good, though.*

JACKIE: *Yes. Okay. I'll be there.* ⟦To Jill⟧ *He told me to bring some toys over . . .*

JILL: *A massager . . .*

JACKIE: *No, I'm not bringing that, because I don't like it in me.*

JILL: *You'll see what he'll do. Like you walk in and sit down normal and he'll tell you a story that he saw in a Swedish whorehouse. In one room, a John came in and then a girl came in. He was a spectator, watching through a one-way mirror . . . like from the other room. And the girl tied the man up, she peed on him, and all this stuff. Like if he tells you this, you gather from what he says that this is what he wants. Then he'll say, "Wait just a minute. I have to get something downstairs." This is a townhouse with three stories. And he'll come back upstairs and knock on the door, and you'll say, "Come in."*

JACKIE: *You pretend it's a whorehouse?*

JILL: *And you pretend he's the John coming in. And you say, "Hello, would you like a cigarette?" and all that bull. He's a real hippie. He'll ask you to smoke a joint. Take a couple, but don't inhale, 'cause he just wants to get you high.*

JACKIE: *How old is he—twenty-six?*

JILL: *He's a little bit older, but he looks real young. He's real nice-looking. He's very rich, but he never works.*

JACKIE: *I'll go along with anything as long as they don't hit me.*

JILL: *Mine don't hit hard!*

⟦Pamela swoops into the living room.⟧

MADAM: *The Admiral just called. I don't know where he gets that name. He says, "I have to have something six feet tall and exotic. By that, he means the biggest boobs you have; 40D if possible. He always says it's for a friend. But the friend has got to mean him.*

Last time he requested a girl thirty-five years old, which is a very unusual request, 'cause that's old in this business. Most guys want the average girl who's

MADAM:	*eighteen, nineteen, or twenty. Which is nothing in bed, of course. But the men themselves have to wake up to that fact after much experience. After they've been through it a few times, they realize the older a girl is, the wiser she is about sex.*
JILL:	*[Interrupting] But she's also ugly.*
MADAM:	*Not so much ugly, unless she's been fucking for a long time.*
JACKIE:	*People say that between twenty-five and thirty-five a girl is best.*
MADAM:	*Well, I just got the Admiral about the closest thing I could find to his specifications. She's only five foot eight. I told her to wear the highest heels possible and a wig on top of her head to add three or four inches. And to do her bust up as best she could—she's only a thirty-eight. That's the best I could do.*
	Then the Admiral calls back when she gets to his apartment. He's sized her up—literally—and says she won't do. All that trouble for nothing. You can't push a girl on a man.

The Men

Pamela: Men are the most interesting and amusing part of the business. When they're in a house, they let their hair down and act like little children. If they're naughty, I know I've succeeded. A man comes in, puts his legs up in a chair, and says, "This is the only place I feel at home."

"But at home, you don't even do that, do you?" I laugh.

"Well, you happen to be right. But I wish I could."

This business is not full of lonely Johns. They're just repressed. Often a man can't talk about his work with his wife. That's a pathetic type. The wife will not share her husband's business interests. It's bad enough she can't satisfy him sexually. She can't even listen. All she wants is a rich executive who brings home the end-of-the-rainbow pot of gold. Money. Money. Money. That's all she wants.

Some men ask: "What am I doing in your house tonight? I guess I'm just another one of the lonely men who come here." But no, no, no. The bigger the executive is, the more he needs a house of joy. Where does he find the time to go out bar hunting? If he's a lawyer, he has to look at his briefs. Or he has to prepare for a conference the next day. He doesn't have time to hunt for a girl, wine and dine her on the hope that he may end up in bed. He probably won't score the first time. For an egomaniac, stalking the prey may be a challenge. But few busy and important men have time to indulge themselves in the chase, so they come to a house.

The girls see one side of his personality. With the girl, he goes to bed. Later, she may say, "Goodness, he was funny. He wanted me to say dirty, dirty words. The more I swear, the more excited he gets. It makes him have a quicker orgasm." She's doing everything his wife doesn't do.

After he balls her, he may take another, prettier girl out for a hundred-dollar dinner date. She's for show, not for sex. But she still must make the man feel that, for the moment, he's the only man in the world. That is the secret of a successful call girl, the secret of a successful madam, and, for that matter, the secret of any woman. Look at Zsa Zsa Gabor.

I let a man free-associate—discuss anything that may cross his mind. He'll say, "You're like my sister. In fact, you look like my sister." While the girls provide sexual solace, I'm a buddy. I listen.

A man will tell me about himself: "I made three hundred fifty thousand after taxes last year. And I paid cash for a Lincoln Continental. I pay fifteen hundred a month for a very fashionable apartment."

That man's showing off. He's nouveau riche. He was born poor and he's happy now—telling me how he feels. I just say, "Keep coming back, darling."

Men frequent different madams, or they may frequent one madam if they like her way of handling people. I have one vice—swearing. I try to note the prudish type: "My goodness. Here comes a banker.

Here comes that real prude of them all. As conservative as hell." I say to the guy who brought him up, "I shouldn't swear in front of him, should I?"

The man says, "Don't you dare. His ears can't take those things."

But honey, we're not the only people who swear today. Legitimate men come up and say, "The fucker, the motherfucker I had in business. What a prostituting cunt he was." Men talk like that.

I say, "What do you mean?"

"He had angles and ulterior motives for everything. He was like a lesbian prostituting cunt. Like that lesbian you had who said she'd never fuck a man for free. That's the kind of businessman he was."

Every type of man you could think of is a John. They all have one thing in common—an ego that has to be inflated. A girl must encourage the man to talk. She must provide comfort. A man doesn't want to hear any problems. In a house, a man wants to forget his conferences and the money his wife wants for this and that.

I love men and sympathize with them. If a man has a bitch, I genuinely sympathize. Say a man has a wife that's fooling around. He knows it, but for the children's sake they stay together. I tell him one thing—one good parent is better than two unhappy parents. Get rid of her and keep the kids.

Actually, I talk business with the men. Rarely do we discuss their personal lives. I know more about business than the wife or secretary. I have a good business head. I know the pros and cons of why the deal was or wasn't made.

The girls have a problem I don't. Every man's goal is to get them out of the business. "What's a girl like you doing in this life?" You get that line all the time. I tell the girls to pull out a picture of the baby—even if they don't have one.

Although I'm a madam, I don't believe a man should want to come to a house of joy. But men come because they treat their wives like china. They'd like, for instance, to make it with their wife and another woman. But they just won't subject their wives to a threesome. *Subject*. That's their word. A man would never end up in a house if he exposed his wife to other sexual pleasures. Phony men say, "You make me love my wife, because she's a real lady." That means straight up and down, alone in bed.

Some men do ask me to introduce their wives to threesomes. They want their women to grow with the times—not to stay at home—silly, stupid, and simple in suburbia. You can't just have a wife read a lot. That's only one type of education.

More men are asking: "Will you expose my wife to a ménage à trois?" I don't recommend making the arrangement at home. Home is sacred. Instead, I send a lesbian to a motel or hotel for a meeting. The wife is usually afraid, but if she loves the man, she'll go along.

The man actually makes the deal. He takes the call girl aside and pays her. His wife doesn't know she's a call girl on call. The initiation is gentle and planned. After the conversion, the man and wife can go to swap parties together and start in the whole wide arena of sexual variety.

A man has to love his wife very much to enlighten her. The man must want to take his wife along with him as he begins to grow and explores new territory.

Swinging

Ten o'clock on a quiet evening at the madam's. Two girls—Joan and Ann—are sitting in. The doorbell rings.

MADAM: *Who is it?*

MAN'S VOICE: *Mike Andrews.*

⟦The madam opens the door and embraces Mike. He is with a young girl.⟧

MADAM·   ⟦Turning to the girls in the living room⟧ *You know everyone in the inner sanctum . . .*

MIKE: *This is Linda and I'm Mike. It's always great to have other people around. Is everybody so quiet here?*

MADAM: *You know Joan and Ann? Joan's Miss Scarsdale. I like to find my nice society girls from the upper crust. So what do you want, Mike? A swapperoo, or something for yourselves?*

⟦Linda is hanging back and shy.⟧

MIKE: *I'm trying to get her interested in Hawaii.*

MADAM: *You're trying to get her interested in another girl?*

ANN: *Isn't Hawaii and another girl one and the same?*

MADAM: *Yeah, if you want it darling. I love that gullible question.*

MIKE: *Let's get inspired by some movies.*

MADAM: *I'll put one on.* ⟦To Linda⟧ *Have you ever been to a swing-a-ding-ding?*

LINDA: ⟦Blurts out⟧ *No.*

MADAM: *Well, a small party would consist of twelve. A swinging party would be approximately thirty. Instead of your bathing suit, you wear your birthday suit.*

LINDA: ⟦Trying to be good-humored⟧ *That's not complicated.*

MADAM: ⟦With a knowing look to Mike⟧ *Especially if you have people who cooperate.*

MIKE: ⟦Looking at the Madam's table photographs⟧ *Gee, you've got the nicest photos.*

MADAM: ⟦Threading the projector⟧ *I'm almost as good as you at putting things in holes, honey. No, that could never be. But I've got balls.*

LINDA: *You should focus a bit.*

MIKE: ⟦Irritated with her lack of enthusiasm⟧ *There's nothing wrong with that. I like the film the way it is.*

MADAM: *It's been precisely six months since I've seen you. We've known each other for umpteen years—too fucking long.*

MIKE: *Sixteen years.*

MADAM: *But it takes six months for you to get around to calling me again, you prick. I know what your bag is. Secretaries. Linda, you're not his secretary, are you?*

LINDA: ⟦Softly⟧ *Not any more.*

MADAM: ⟦Ignoring Linda and addressing Mike⟧ *'Cause if you were, you wouldn't be anymore. That's what I say. I'm telling you for your own sake.* ⟦Mike laughs

MADAM: nervously.] *He gets hung up on secretaries. I shouldn't tell secrets out of school. But I know why I haven't seen him for six months. Secretaries. He gets involved.*

MIKE: [Irritated] *Not her. Not anymore.*

MADAM: *Was she the one that wanted to have a baby for you? Who could forget that? She didn't care if she had the baby without a father either. "I want a child by you." So dramatic.*

MIKE: *Linda has had very little experience.*

MADAM: *In other words, you just leaf it over to another chapter? I'm more of a promiscuous fuck than you could ever be.*

MIKE: *Are you kidding? You're the greatest.*

MADAM: *I don't settle for one at a time—girls or boys.*

MIKE: *Have you gotten involved in anything lately?*

MADAM: *Just arranging things for the likes of you. Hey, let's start another film. I get bored with these pictures. Not enough tricks in them. I like lots of men around.*

MIKE: [Now taking note of the film of two girls and a man] *Linda, just think of what that girl could do to you?*

LINDA: [Sarcastic and resentful] *What could she do to you!*

MADAM: *Why don't you kids adjourn? Here's Joan.* [Turns to Joan] *Could I have a conference with you?*

MADAM: [Aside to Joan] *He wants you to go in with them both and make it with her while he's making it with you. Concentrate on her.*

[Joan returns to the couch.]

JOAN: *There's room for three of us on the couch, Mike. Here are some stories.* [She pulls out photographic magazines with pictures of threesomes.]

MIKE: *Oh, that's just it. Look at this, Linda.*

[Linda turns her head away.]

JOAN: [Enthusiastic] *Here's another story, honey.*

MIKE: *These are terrific. Don't you like them, Linda?*

MADAM: [*To Linda*] *You've been here an hour. Make up your mind, honey. I want to get this girl for you.* [Linda is reticent; the madam continues to Mike] *Come here and talk to me. I don't want to shock my own house.*

[Mike and the Madam go into the kitchen.]

MADAM: *You've been up here for a while, and I don't have social visits in this place. So get going—into the bedroom or out.*

MIKE: *Take it easy. This is Linda's first time. I think I can get her to go.*

MADAM: *Christ, you take up people's time when you need two hours to decide!*

MIKE: [Returns to couch and picks up picture of a man and woman together] *Linda, I like this picture. But it's missing one thing. It should be two girls and a guy. Three's company. Two is routine. Are you ready?*

LINDA: *To go in?*

MADAM: *He happens to be right. Two's nothing.*

MIKE: *Two's just the beginning of fun.*

MADAM: *You come all the way up here. That's just the beginning of fun. Come on, Linda honey.*

[Linda is silent.]

MADAM: *You can't just sit around and take your time like this, sweetheart.*

MIKE: *We going to make movies tonight?*

MADAM: *You want to go into the skinflick business?*

MIKE: *I'll be in them.*

MADAM: *Well, you're in advertising and you have the power of persuasion. You could educate people to share the joy.*

[Mike drinks a toast to the madam.]

MIKE: *To the greatest woman I know.*

MADAM: *I'm in the wrong game, though.*

MIKE: *Oh no you're not.*

MADAM: *Well, I am, until I go public.*

MIKE: *Honey, you've been public ever since I've known you. Hey, put a little water in my drink. It's too strong. It gives me a headache.*

MADAM: ⟦Looking at Linda⟧ *Some girls around here give me a headache.* ⟦To Mike⟧ *I'll give you a backrub and a massage. It's just as good as coming. Sometimes better.*

MIKE: *You have your backrub and I'll have my coming!*

MADAM: *Coming you can have anytime. You need the backrub more.*

MIKE: *Rub me in the right place and I'll go.*

MADAM: *You pervert. Sex you can get anytime. I still go for love. Linda goes for love too. She's not spoiled yet.*

LINDA: ⟦Relieved that the madam has changed her tack⟧ *You're right.*

MIKE: ⟦To madam⟧ *How about you? You'd be great with a girl.*

MADAM: *Not working tonight. But I do "Have girl, will travel."*

MIKE: *Linda'll get into this.*

MADAM: *I don't underestimate the shy little quiet ones. She's game, baby. I know she's game.*

MIKE: ⟦Referring to Linda⟧ *This one?*

MADAM: *Once. Try it once. And if you don't like it, just don't do it again.*

⟦MIKE: Gently⟧ *You willing to try, Linda?*

⟦A very long, sad silence.⟧

MADAM: ⟦Irritated⟧ *You said before she'd never do this.*

MIKE: ⟦Angry, grabs Linda by the arm and picks up their coats⟧ *Okay. I give up. Let's get going.*

JOAN: *Just give me one long kiss, Mike. We can't ruin your whole evening!*

MIKE: *Here's a special.*

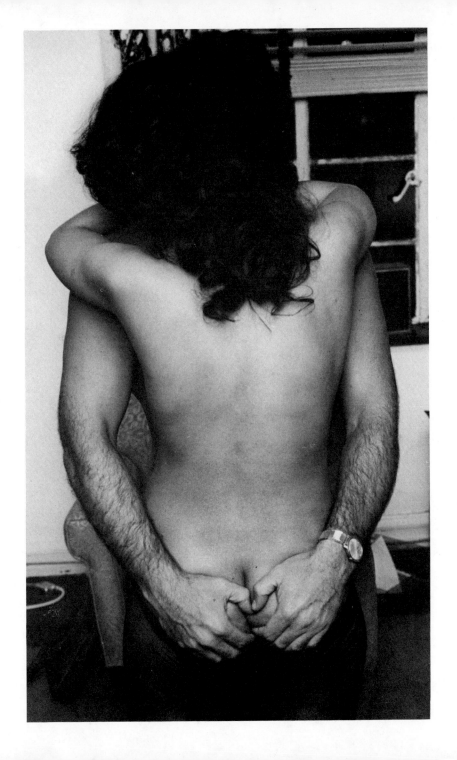

Specials

PAMELA: Men come to the house and want specialties. I've got an old man I call "Cock-a-doodle-do." He likes five girls dressed in peacock feathers to run around with their hands up in the air like wings—saying, "Cock-a-doodle-do." He's so old he can't get it up, but everytime he heard that little word—*c-o-c-k*—what do you think he's doing with his hands? One, two, three, jerking off.

Some men like facials and make a girl take a suppository first. Or they ask that she not douche after her last customer. One man, who kept a monkey in his own home to have the smell around, had a fetish for odors. I can't figure him out.

Phone freaks call to have me speak dirty. This is by far the simplest way to make money. I've probably met the man under ordinary circumstances, and, at first he's afraid to let his special wishes out. But when he does, I come to an arrangement with him and just talk when he calls. I get different girls to carry on conversations, because this kind of man has a fascination for different women saying different words. Each girl fulfills a separate fantasy. The day after the call, I get a check or money order in the mail. Wouldn't you like the phone to ring and know there'll be a check for fifty or a hundred in the mail the next day?

I provide many fantasy services. A man might come up at four in the morning and be a slave. One girl puts out the dog food; she makes him crawl around and eat it. She whips his ass if he doesn't. Someone else will then make him do housework. All the while, he's panting, hot, and happy.

One very wealthy department-store owner comes up with yards of velvet to be measured for a robe. This man never undresses. You never do anything to him. It's all in his imagination. Just stand before the mirror pinning material and he's in paradise.

He likes to pretend you're very rich and that you're going to kidnap him. He says, "Do you have a country home?" You're supposed to answer yes. One girl actually took him to someone's country place, where she kept him for three weeks. She just made sure he had his checkbooks. He signed checks for fifteen thousand dollars. After this girl actually got him, his family put a private detective on his tail, so he's harder to nail now.

I don't play the sadomasochistic game, because it's dangerous. These men have orgasms when you hit them, beat them, and stampede them with boots. They pay two hundred and up, so it's very lucrative, but a man can turn on *you.*

I avoid Negroes as clients. Not because they're black, but because they're associated with dope. Margaret Mead prefers marijuana to cigarettes, but she can have it till it's legalized. I do keep amil-nitrate around. It's a medication for heart disease. If you break it open and rub it on a man's nose just before he comes, he gets oozy and has a way-out feeling. But that's about as far as I'll go with dope.

The main problem with men is credit. If you take a check, and the man is drunk, he may stop payment the next morning.

A top Italian from Brooklyn wanted credit. He was probably backed by the boys, because he said constantly, "You want a contract?" That statement just ripped out of the side of his mouth. "Anytime you want a contract, just call me."

One day he was stoned out of his mind, and he didn't even have a bank check on him. He couldn't remember his account number. I said, "No credit." He pulled a gun. I pulled a crying spree: "God, God is my only friend at this moment." I was really frightened, but suddenly he put the gun away and left.

The next day he came back and apologized—on his knees. He threw a lot of money at me and begged to come back in my good graces. Which proves again who needs who more. I don't need the men, but they need services only *I* can provide.

The same men may frequent different madams. Or they may frequent one madam if they like her way of handling people. It's a very personal business. You'd be surprised how many men enjoy my sarcastic and surly way.

It's actually illegal for a man to come to a prostitute. Once only prostitution itself was illegal, so a man could easily turn a girl in. That's one reason why girls—not just streetwalkers and colored girls

—cater to the cloak-and-suiters and to Chinese people. These men would never turn a girl in. The cloak-and-suiters need their services too badly and the Chinese are just plain nice and honest.

The Judge

Eleven o'clock. Two customers have just been hastened out the door. The madam awaits a restaurant owner, who's bringing up a Criminal Court judge for a treat. The doorbell rings. The men have arrived.

MADAM: *Hi, Lenny. Hello, judge. I'd like you to meet Betsy and Vicky.*

JUDGE: [Laughing] *I'm going to put you all in jail.*

MADAM: *Oh bullshit. I had a big senator here last week. It doesn't matter who you are. You come here and you're in another world. You drink scotch, darling? Serve him scotch, Betsy. It's all ready.*

JUDGE: *Scotch and water.*

MADAM: *Sit down and make yourself uncomfortable. Betsy's on your left, Vicky on the right. Lenny, you want a drink, dear?*

LENNY: *I'm going to have to go, my dear. But I want to talk to you for one second.*

MADAM: *Uno momento.*

LENNY: *Judge, will you excuse me for a minute?*

[Lenny and the Madam go into a huddle to make the business arrangements for the judge's treat. Betsy prepares drinks at the bar and the cabinet door falls off.]

BETSY: *Oh, I did something wrong.*

JUDGE: *What'd you do? Break it?*

BETSY: *No, I think it comes off the track.*

JUDGE: *Do you?*

BETSY: *No. Not much. You think you've seen me before? You been a judge long?*

JUDGE: *Three years.*

BETSY: *Sentence a lot of people?*

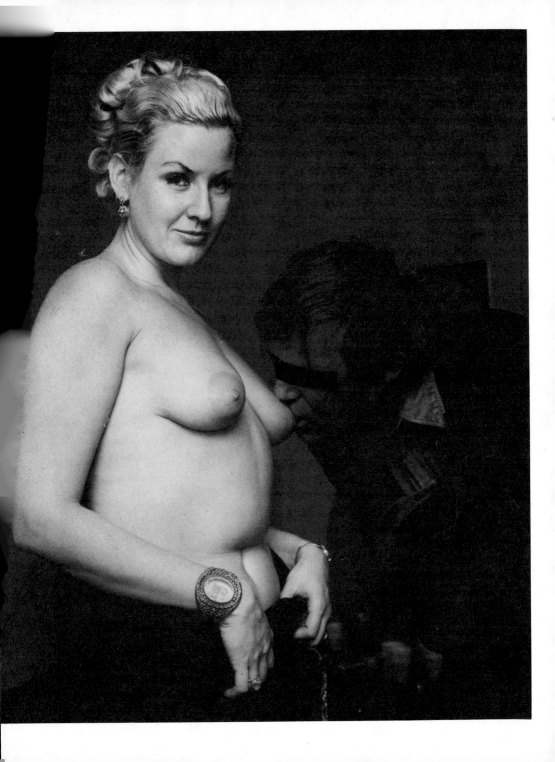

JUDGE: *Yeah. Certain cases I'm very rough on. Certain cases don't matter. Come sit on my lap.*

〚Betsy comes over and plunks herself down.〛

JUDGE: *Gambling I'm not hard on. Unless I tell the guy to cut it out for a while and he keeps coming back.*

BETSY: 〚*Stroking his ear*〛 *Yeah?*

JUDGE: *Then he's asking for it.*

BETSY: 〚*Seductive*〛 *So are you!*

〚Vicky has started a film.〛

BETSY: *This film is wild!*

JUDGE: *I prefer it live. This film is ridiculous. Anyway, it's pornographic and illegal.*

BETSY: *What are you going to do about it?*

JUDGE: *Confiscate it and you. In fact, there's a memo out— parole all cases you can. If the girl is stupid, she jumps bail, or she jumps parole. They parole most prostitutes, but if they don't show up, they put warrants on them.*

VICKY: *So you've just got to show up.*

BETSY: *I've thought about lying.*

JUDGE: *Let me tell you something. If you lie, you get perjury and that's five years. Now which would you rather have—five years or fifteen days?*

VICKY: *Postponement. That's what I'm for.*

JUDGE: *I hope not now! Let's go.*

The Raid

NOTE: Every girl who worked for the madam thought she was protected. The madam had told me she paid the cops in her precinct. Part of the fifty-percent cut she takes from the girls covers police protection. When the house was raided, everyone had a different version of the mistake or mismanagement.

The madam blamed Lisa, who got angry when Pamela threw her out of the house for mistreating a client. She thought Lisa had gone and squealed to the cops. Ruth thought Lisa had squealed too. But she thought Lisa had good reason. The madam had abused her and screamed at her.

Maggie was working at the madam's house when the raid began.

M AGGIE: I'd been sitting in the living room between two plain-clothesmen. I was talking to them about absolutely nothing—where they worked and what they did. But I got very bad vibrations from these guys. It's a sensitivity awareness that I have. I knew in my very utter soul a bad feeling. If I had touched one of them, felt his body from head to toe, I would have found his gun. Then I would have said, "Hey, man, keep cool. You want to make it here? You want to bust the joint? Just let me out of here, 'cause I don't want any part of it." If he was any kind of cop, he would have stayed cool and let me go. But thinking this is an afterthought.

The two plainclothesmen went off with the madam to negotiate. Later they said I was negotiating, but I didn't say a word. After settling with Pamela, one of them opened the door and called the captain, standing in the stairwell. I could see him from the couch. The captain came in; a lieutenant followed. We all got shook up. Did you ever tremble? Panic? Well, you go through shit. Your heart throbs and the blood starts soaring through your body. You're vibrating heat waves.

When Pamela came in, she couldn't believe it. She says, "Oh, officer, you've got to be kidding. Be serious." She'd meanwhile been telling us girls that everything was cool and taken care of. There'd be no problems.

One customer was in the bedroom. The policeman asked, "Do you come here often?"

The guy said, "Yeah."

"Schmuck," said the cop. The customer should have taken us out. Just one human being to another. He could have said, "These are my girlfriends and I'm taking them out to dinner." Just denied this was a madam's house. But he didn't.

We all sat there while the cops tore the place apart. They took out all the phones for evidence. Some of the girls had to change their clothes or get into clothes. They took us down in the elevator and I wanted to run. I thought, "What would they do if I ran? Beat me? Shoot me?" I was too chickenshit to run. I wish I'd known karate. I could have gotten away. The cops weren't about to shoot whores.

We were herded down to the precinct, where all the cops stared at us like milk cows. Fortunately, I had someone sleeping over with my children. When we got to the precinct, I called my brother to tell him the truth. He hadn't known I was in this business. There was dead silence on the telephone, and then he said, "Are you all right? Did anybody hurt you?"

I said, "Don't worry. I'll go through it. It's probably a physical ordeal more than anything else."

The cop was typing away at ten sheets and little cards. He's typing away and digging typing. I was putting this cop on. I gave him a phony name and business address. When you get busted for the first time, they don't check on anything in your handbag, except for drugs and sharp objects. I tell this guy, "Okay. I'm going to punch you right in the cock. I'm not going to take this." It was funny, because he was uptight and I was show biz.

When I was having my picture taken, the cop said, "All right, look forward." I blew up my cheeks like a blowfish. I did a profile of the same thing. The guy said, "Do us cops get a discount?"

"If you fuck your mother, you can get a discount."

Everytime I related to someone—whether it was a captain or a lieutenant, a detective, a patrolman, an officer—male or female—I reached out to them as one human being to another. Not what their badge was. Not what their color was, but basically as a human person. I am a very humanistic woman.

Later, at around five in the morning, we had to go to another precinct to a cell, before we were taken to the courthouse. The cell had an open toilet pit and a sink. What a smell! But I figured I'd lie down and get some sleep, just rest my body. I was so tired and had the whole next day to wait for court.

They came by and asked if I wanted coffee. I got a delicious bagel, but the coffee was from a cesspool. I thought they wanted to poison me.

There were dope addicts in the next cell. I heard them talk about their trips and how they got busted. When a new girl would come in, someone would say, "Oh gee, I haven't seen you in a long time." Very, very sad.

I was lying there thinking. I said to myself: What am I doing this for? My kids are eleven, ten, nine, eight, and seven. My children are my jewels and my reward in life. I'm doing this to support them.

The sound image in the cell when you sit on the john is like a hellish nightmare. It's such a bad sound—like suction, whirring. The loud vibrating sound of the toilet bowl sucking you down into the abyss of hell. It was like we all had our little hell holes right in the cell, and, when we pressed the button, we could hear ourselves being sucked into Hades. I'm sensitive to sounds and rhythms, so that toilet bowl was really shit.

Finally the cops are ready to take you downtown. You haven't had a moment's sleep. You walk past all these fucking cops—"Hey baby, you got some discount rates for us?" Looking you over and passing snide remarks.

I walked out to the van with some dope addicts and saw this cop who I'd gone to high school with. I pulled down my hat and he didn't recognize me, but my heart fell out.

We went in the back door at the courthouse and wound through the halls. It was "Merrily we roll along" like kids—hopping, skipping, jumping, and turning corners. Finally we get to this very large cell—the zoo. There were a mass of bull-dyke cops, but they do their job and don't mess with you. Ninety-seven percent of the chicks in the cell are streetwalkers with wigs and boots. They're trying to get some sleep.

I talked to a streetwalker I knew had a pimp. She said that she was devoting three years of her life to the street and she didn't care about the busts because the money was so good.

I said, "You're living in hell. I dig watching 'Laugh-In,' 'David Frost,' or just doing nothing some nights. How can you do it, getting hassled? It's a really rough life." But she just tells me how she rolls drunks and tries to avoid the cops. She says she actually has fun!

The streetwalker is the toughest kind of prostitute in the world. She's made of another thing. Some element that doesn't chemically exist. She has stamina and fortitude above and beyond middle-class America. Maybe because she's from the lower class. Higher-class chicks don't walk the street, because it's a whole different existence.

You just sit in the zoo until they call you to court. I read the writing on the wall. "Sonny and John forever." The love affairs. Also, "Right on," and "Power to the People." The ventilation is terrible and everyone is smoking. There were lots of junkies. One girl—her arms, her legs, her whole body was a mass of swollen puffiness. No veins anymore. One by one, as the day went on, the old black women junkies came in. I felt sorrier for the junkies than any girl who walks the streets. It's a compulsive addiction that drives them.

I began to think: Maybe the streetwalker is an addict too. It isn't nymphomania. It's another drive that goes to a deep psychological root. Everyone has a need to drive them on—an obsession. A pimp compels the streetwalker. And the streetwalker is compelled to the pimp because she has a need to be loved and cared for. The need to be loved drove me into this business. I derive a sense of love from mastery over the situation. I like the power of being master. I can control a man when I'm in bed with him. I've learned to put him absolutely in my hands and make him do my every whim and wish. Even though he's paying me, my sexuality and sensuality place him in my sphere, so if he tries to screw me, I can turn the tables on him.

Some women's liberationists were brought to the zoo. They came in saying, "Power to the people," and I told them to shut up, because I was so upset. I'd been waiting for six hours in the zoo. The cops give you sandwiches, but forget the paper they call bread.

The women's liberationists asked if I had an attorney, and, if I didn't, they'd get me one. That was a human consideration. A human connection.

We were finally taken to the courtroom and I felt all the eyes on me. I felt heavy, because so many people seemed to be there just to stare. I was released on bail for a hearing, but I want to get my records back and have them destroyed. This won't happen to me again, and I don't want a blotch on my life.

I got out of the courthouse and walked through the revolving door and looked up at the great big building. I started to get emotional and tears swelled up in my eyes. I cried and ran and cried. People were looking at me, but I couldn't believe how excited I was to be free. I was out of the cage. I was out of the zoo. I was out of the humiliating circumstances.

I went to have a hot dog, just like eight million other people in the city. I was a human being again. I ran to a phone booth and turned into my natural self and called home. My brother said everything was okay—he'd been watching the kids and they had enough food. Everyone was pulling together for me, which was a nice feeling. But I was physically and mentally wiped out.

INDIVIDUAL ENTREPRENEURS

Maggie

CHAPTER FOUR

INDIVIDUAL
ENTREPRENEURS

MAGGIE
After the Madam

MAGGIE: I never went back to the madam's after that raid.
I just never called. By now, I've got plenty of my own lists
and contacts. I can play it cool and count on myself. I certainly
wouldn't risk going to jail ever again!

Girls say that it's safe to work for a madam. You're
protected, because a madam has to be in with the law to stay
in business. I learned my lesson fast. The only guarantee in
this business is yourself. The city gets hot and so does every
working girl—madam or me. You are your own security.
Keep what you do to yourself and no one can touch you.

MAGGIE: Hey I was lucky today. I got off the bus and nobody attacked me. No molesters. No exhibitionists. I couldn't believe it. Then I had a tripleheader. I was in a warehouse with over a million dollars of raw mink. We did a square dance and from that, went to a polka. I just took care of the customers. People pay you for a service and you service them—like Texaco. Today there were three men. One blow job, and the other two killed me. They were all the way, but it was easy, 'cause I douched with Scope.

Only two things were satisfying. I got money and I got a piece of fur. Everytime I see these guys, I pick up another piece of lamb—died and electrified lamb. Really beautiful. Within a year, I'll have a coat. My bonus. They give me lamb like the cab fare home.

I live in Brooklyn in a house. Eight rooms and one fifty a month rent. My walls are painted blue. I love blue and green. My bedroom is done in gold dust and alligator-cracked walls. Utter chaos. I'm hoping, if I can put together enough money, my decorator (Yeah, I have a decorator!) and I will buy some inexpensive panelings and put together a room for me. My five children's rooms—they're in genuine need of painting and work. Sporadic painting I do, but never completing the job.

I've had a lot of kids and I've gone through a lot of shit. I wasn't a very good housekeeper. I wasn't very good at being a mother. I'm impatient and flamboyant. I just have too much personality for a mother. All of a sudden, I had a great big H-bomb explode inside me. I didn't want my husband any more. It wasn't working. I said to myself, "Leave. Make it on your own." But I didn't realize how weak I was.

My husband assisted me very modestly. I'm quite sure, even if he was well off, he wouldn't help. He still has a mental block, an emotional hangup he can't overcome. He can't give. He thinks I was the major catastrophe in his life. With *his* five children. I had to go on public assistance and his meager support.

I got myself a regular job, but that wasn't enough money. Then I started whoring on the side. I did it out of basic poverty. But working all day and then putting up with the aggravation all night—that was too hectic. I never saw the kids. So I went back to the root of all evil full time. I've been a straight whore ever since.

If you keep up with this goddamn life on a steady diet, day and night, with a break in the morning and back to it—fucking and business and nothing but that, you can easily break. Girls seek release through drinking and pills and dexies and upsies and downsies. Whatever. I haven't had to. I can be self-destructive without destroying myself. I'm masochistic, but I can live with it. I can go about my daily routine and not let it suck me up.

Like men are nice to your face—sweet and complimentary. You turn your back and overhear: "You cunt." That cuts. I didn't think I could take it till I started. It's difficult, but I'm cool the way I am. I don't work every day. Some days it rains; I stay home.

You could let bad talk bother you. Then you can't sleep and you start to propel yourself to one thing—money, money, money. That's all that's important. What's really important is to reach the top people—the most successful, affluent, giving people. If you make an effort, you can be lucky to meet the right people—financial-wise.

Let's say you have a hidden flare for business, or you're artistically inclined. If you meet just the right money person and they believe in you, you can go into that endeavor. It *can* happen. I've got to believe.

It's all called playing the game. You want to meet better people so you don't have to go out that much and still make almost the same money. If not more.

Playing the game is fantastic. It's like being on stage and anticipating your fellow actors. I'm always one step ahead of the motherfucker. I don't want to come out the loser. I won't be upstaged. If you stay ahead, the man doesn't try to con and bullshit you and waste your time. Your time is precious; it's money. You don't want to be bothered. "Call me. Fine. We'll make an arrangement." Have a business deal. I don't want to believe in a man beyond that.

I used to believe everybody. I was a celebrity fucker. I never cast cocks in plaster, but I think that's beautiful. I found out actors come on heavy and drop you like a dishrag: "Get away, little girl." They don't have use for you after a lay, so I gave that up. I don't trust anybody anymore.

Men pay and I perform. Some men are completely obnoxious. I dislike them because they're repulsive. I can't stand their smell. I can't stand their personality. I just don't want to be with them, 'cause I get such bad vibrations.

One real Mafiosa type—I had to tie him and whip him. Taunt him. A real sicky. But as sick as he was, I became as sick as he was. You automatically label yourself in the deeper recesses of your cerebrum—that you're as sick as the man. The whole thing's a sick game. You have to be on a super plateau—constantly cooling off your guilt and saying, "It's okay. It's good."

I want to be a supersexy lady. Cool. Funny. I'd like to say nothing to the world. I'd like to be Desdemona and Delilah. If you're going to play a stupid game, why not play a classy one?

Generally, I like the work. I've built up a big book of customers and work off my phone. Some people I do get good vibrations with. You tell the man, "Look. I'm here to please you." Once he knows he's king, he's going to have a great deal of pride and respect, because you put him on a tremendous plateau. You don't rush him like a honky-tonk. You have a bit of class.

I get a marvelous sense of power. This comes from the sexual act itself. As a woman, I feel strength when I feel sexual power. I never felt that way when I was married. I didn't know what a woman was supposed to be like. What a real woman is. I've learned to experience a climax. What it is to be tender and warm and understanding. Affectionate. Humanistic. Compassionate. Everyone I meet basically likes me. I have a bit of hostility on one side, but on the other is this warmth and goodness. "Hey, I like you," men say. "That's really very nice."

Then I'm in control—like I'm a pilot. I press the buttons and man the ship. The sense of control is control over the cock. I love that power. It turns me on. I get turned on too by men with hundred-dollar bills. Lots of them.

One Chinamen with two hundreds was superduper. Supersexually driven by some force. He needed to express himself. I was the earth he took it out on. I was the only planet he was in touch with. But the second time I saw him, it didn't happen. He was charming and nice and I just wanted to get away from him.

Sometimes I have climaxes. Some men just do a great job. They eat me and I let myself go. I say, "I'm going to come. I'm going to take. That man's a giver. Give him a Purple Heart and a gold star." Let him do his job and I come up saying, "You're too good. You're the greatest." I just give in. Then my legs tremble all the way home.

Other times I have to act. I love the theater in my heart. The Stanislavsky method I use at work has saved me from cracking up—emotionally and mentally. Sometime, I'll try acting out of bed!

I do feel guilty about my current performances. That comes from somewhere in the guts. Somewhere in the lower abdomen, there's a guilt that lasts for a second and then goes.

The money I make from prostitution is psychologically, unconsciously bad money. I hate it. I splurge with it. But I'm so guilty when I rush to buy something for the kids? Ha.

All this time, I'm going to see a psychiatrist on my welfare. He's a schmuck on Park Avenue—nodding off to sleep while I talk. "Oh, yes." "Oh, no." "What did you say?" He's asked me for a couple of numbers of other girls for himself. He doesn't give two shits about me as a human being. He just collects that welfare check.

The doctor said that for me to resort to this going out and getting money from men—it means it was always in me. I would have done it somehow or other, even if I didn't get divorced. There's a need in me for self-destruction. I was going to self-destruct, one way or another, because I'm masochistic.

My doctor thinks I'm very strong. I have gained strength in all the shit that's gone on in the years since I left my husband. I have gained in stature. The doctor is trying to help me realize why I got myself into prostitution and how to accept what I do. He knows he can't reform me.

I've learned to recognize my basic drives for self-destruction. I can see I fulfill them in my work. This gives me an odd contentment.

Every girl who goes through this routine is destructive. Some can enjoy it. Others can't.

My real problem is my boyfriend. I've seen him for a year. It's hard to play the goddamn game away from him and then come back and be real. Chaotic and unreal; that's me. I am straight with my boyfriend, but he doesn't know what I do and it's difficult to make explanations. I tell him I've had a date with a few other friends; that they're well off and I go to fine restaurants. I never demand that *he* take me to the finest clubs. I've never asked for jewelry. I never would. We do have a great time intimately, because my boyfriend knows me. He knows the reasons I act the way I do—when I'm putting him on and when I'm being a child. Most of all, he knows me when I'm being supersexy. He digs me, because I'm bawdy— like Tom Jones in a capsule. But he is a cold person; I might just like him because he rejects me deep down.

One thing I can say good about myself—and this goes for me as a girlfriend and as a whore—I'm a very sensual person. I dig people for the instant chemical transfer and emotional reaction. If I dig someone, I go to bed right away. I don't wait and think.

I was playing the game straight for years. I wasn't going out to ball for money. I was getting nowhere, man. Then I said, "I have bills to pay. What kind of self-respect do I have for being a swinger? I put out for one guy because he's good-looking and he uses his knee in one way, so I'm going to drop my pants for him?" I decided to work with a will and goal, instead of fucking around.

Prostitution may not be legal, but it is certainly legitimate. Business would crumble without it. Every industry in the world—manufacturing, import, export—every business would collapse if businessmen didn't use prostitution as a manipulating means of entertaining, a method of increasing sales and pacifying clients. A prostitute is just an instrument for Mr. X who's got a million-dollar corporation and has to do business with Mr. Y. We consummate deals. We're like a barter system. In fact, we're like money. Our backs are the bridges which link business deals.

I prostitute myself with my own business goals. This summer I have visions of working part time. I'm going to buy a hot-dog cart and an ice-cream cart and keep them in a stand-in truck which I'll drive around Brighton. The truck will let me go off for weekends with the kids.

I'll take the kids to a commune. I dig people in communes. They're quiet and gentle. They're genuine. They don't expect anything from you. They share their grass, their food, and their bed.

INDIVIDUAL ENTREPRENEURS

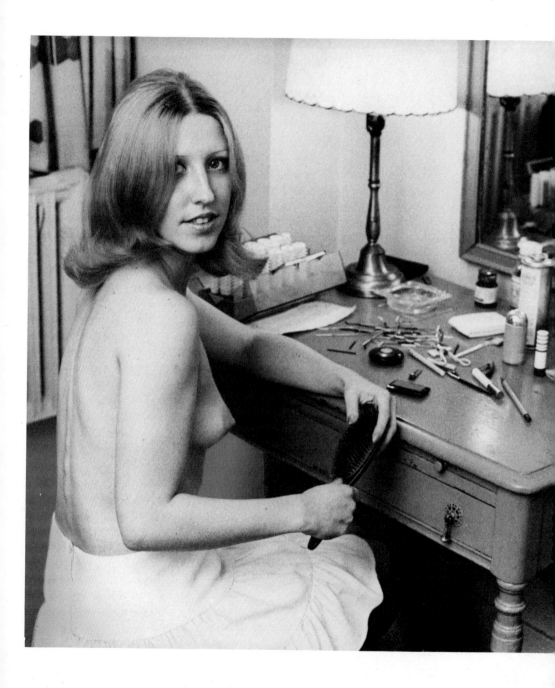

INDIVIDUAL ENTREPRENEURS

$\mathcal{R}UT\mathcal{H}$
a Freelancer

NOTE: Ruth was one of ten children—the only girl. She was brought up near New York in a close family environment and, by her own report, had always lived a "hippy-ish" existence. Her enthusiams were fresh, her experiences new, and she had great hopes of "sharing" and "caring"—her definitions of sex—with the many men she met.

Ruth was a Catholic, but she didn't have to whore for six days a week and pray for redemption on Sunday. She was shrewd enough to take the Bible and fit it to her new way of life.

RUTH: I'm twenty-two, just an old hag in this work. When I was sixteen, I thought taking money for sex was bad and evil. Then I realized we pay taxes, which is the same thing. Here we are paying the country for its grace in allowing us to live here—which is wrong. But the world is set up on a monetary basis. Clothes are for sale; that isn't right. I think everyone should share and give, but that just isn't the way it works. Everything is done for money in the good old USA. You have to fit into society. You can't be as rebellious as these kids, because, if you fight the system, sooner or later you're going to be destroyed by it.

One summer, when I was younger, I lived on a beach in a tent. I had a Johnny Appleseed existence. I fished and hunted and lived off the land. Eight of us had a little community on a beach on Long Island. We traded fish for vegetables and built our camp fires and cooked. But it didn't work. Outsiders put pressure on us. Parents came down and picketed where we were living. They thought we were evil and wrong—boys and girls mixed together, living out in the wilderness. They couldn't understand that things God put there for us to use were being wasted. When the sun comes up in the morning, it's its own special kind of miracle. People teach you to believe this when you're little; when you get older, they teach you to disbelieve.

I started to do the usual things. I went to college and got a bachelor's degree in biochemistry and marine biology. In seven years, I'll start to use that degree, but I wanted money now. So I worked as a go-go dancer in the Catskills. I had offers to go to bed with men for money constantly. I did have sex with a different guy every night, but I just didn't feel like doing it for money. I made around fifty dollars a night dancing, and I preferred to relax with younger guys who couldn't, or wouldn't pay. Then I decided I was going to be extremely rich.

My boyfriend, who I'd been going with for about a year, had met a madam at a swap party and he introduced her to me. Working as a prostitute was the first idea I'd had. I made the decision on my own. My boyfriend didn't influence me and he certainly doesn't benefit from the money I get. I put it all in investments for the future.

He's very rich and in his third year of law school. He has to work hard, so we don't see each other too often. We'll have lunch almost every day and he calls at least eight times. We don't sleep together much, because, when we do, we like to spend the whole night together and our schedules don't merge any more. My boyfriend understands that my need to make money and meet people would come out sooner or later. It's easier to have my work out in the open between us. I say, "This is what I'm doing for a living, and if you don't like it, at least you know." My boyfriend happens to be into swinging and swapping, so his mind is more open. When you swap, you get rid of jealousy. In the beginning, I couldn't stand to watch him with other women. I just wanted to walk out of the room, because I was so jealous. Then I adjusted. My being with other men doesn't bother him either. People who swing and women in this business make good marriages, because jealousy is eliminated.

My boyfriend still pays for all my clothes and my rent. The money I make from work is just for playthings and investments. Money is important to me, because I want to be very lazy. Now I rent ski chalets for two thousand a season. I want to own race-horse stables and get an interest in an advertising agency. This all takes big money —the kind I can make in this business.

Everyone in my family knows what I do. My brothers are defensive, because they want to protect me and they worry about my safety. They have no moral feelings and they think the money's great. My father's figured out that once I want to do something, I'll do it whether he likes it or not. Since I'm not living with him, he's got no control over me. My father sets up only one regulation: "If you are happy in what you are doing, and you're not ashamed of yourself, then it can't be wrong."

Reach out. That is my motto. I like to touch. I like to feel. I really like to meet people. If someone on the street says, "Hello," I stop and talk to them for half an hour.

I care. That's my specialty. It's a real rarity. Sex is part of caring and the reason you have sex with someone is because, in one way or another, you care. You may care about a man because he's improving you financially, or because he's helping you out. You can care about him for no logical reason at all. It can just relax your senses. You do what you want on the moment. What you do on the moment is right. "I care today, because today is today. Maybe tomorrow I won't care, but I'm not going to make up my mind now whether I'll care tomorrow. I'll make up my mind tomorrow."

Caring is, of course, a minor emotion. Loving is a very strong emotion. Basically, you can love one person and you should care about everyone. Marriage-type love should include only one person. But if you *care* about one person, you're leading a very limited life. It's impossible to say, "I only care about you and nobody else I meet makes any difference to me." Everybody you meet makes a difference and formulates your life style.

If you want to count as boyfriends people I see and sleep with now, it's nine or ten. I have only one love who I tell what I'm feeling and doing. With the rest, it's a brother-sister relationship.

I went out to Long Island to visit old friends who'd been in the band I danced with. I stayed with six guys and cared about all of them. It was a small house with wall-to-wall mattresses. I visited for the whole weekend and slept with all but one. He was colored, and I've got a strong thing against that. I believe that God made a difference in people for a reason, and if there wasn't a reason, there wouldn't be any differences. I believe in God's differences.

The Bible tells you to love only one person, but to care about every person—you should make every man your brother. Sex is a strong part of brotherhood, because it's a strong part of today. The way I live, the laws against incest should be abolished!

I show emotion physically. I'm a very outdoor person and walk around saying, "I care, I care." Now there's the old story of the high-school kid talking to his girlfriend. He says, "If you love me, prove it." There's something in that. It doesn't work when you're a kid of fourteen, because you can't feel anything and your ideas aren't strong enough. But as you get older, sex and emotion melt together. That's what I've found working. I can express myself in bed.

I started at a madam's, but then launched out on my own, because the madam was screaming at all her girls. "Nobody does anything. Nobody cares about me."

I said, "A week ago, I did all your business. I answered the phone, I was in the house day and night. I fetched your dog."

She said, "Nobody cares about me."

"Three strikes and you're out," I replied. "That's an old rule." She screamed at one of the other girls. This girl got all upset and went to the bathroom to throw up while the madam is still yelling. I said, "Shut up. Will you shut up. I can't take it any more."

"Don't tell me to shut up. Make me shut up." I slugged her right in the mouth. I smacked her as hard as I could and she hollered, "Get out, get out. Nobody cares about me." I just left.

Now I've got my own business. One man I met at the madam's is giving me business. I also picked up two guys from Wall Street who send customers. I met a man at a straight modeling studio and he gave me forty names to call on my own. I'm protected, because I know the people who send me business. They, in turn, send me people they know. I've made four or five good business connections. It's easier than giving a madam her forty percent, and a lot cheaper too.

One of my friends manages a hostess agency. She runs a legitimate organization for big shows and office parties, but she does have guys who call up, "Have you got a girl who'll sleep with me?"

She says, "Yes, I know a girl, but it's not with this business, so keep your mouth shut." This puts money in my pocket, although she takes a bit of a cut—twenty-five percent.

I also do witchcraft cults where only thirteen people are allowed. Everyone at the orgy is a representative of the devil and you can have mass sex. It's an elaborate ritual with altars and black candles and incense. People run around in black and white robes. I like the ceremony of offering yourself to Satan.

I've been clearing about twelve hundred a week on my own. I've got a book that's huge and I love all the men in it. Men in this business are so nice. I just met a man who's recently divorced and very lonely. He's giving me six months to fall in love with him, and, if

I don't, he's going to marry me anyway. In the past three weeks, I've gotten three proposals of marriage.

I do like men better than women. Women always put on big airs about the things they do. Most girls in the business won't admit they're call girls. When someone asks me, I say, "I'm a call girl and it's a good business. Probably the best around. If Ruth in the Bible could be one, why can't I? I perform an important service. Men can't do business if they're unhappy. And I make businessmen happy."

I feel that I'm doing good work. I perform a service while following my natural instincts. I don't always get tremendous personal, sexual satisfaction from my work, but there's a mental satisfaction from helping people. What I do does seem perfectly natural.

Prostitution is illegal, but that's illegal and unconstitutional. Technically, in this country, you have the right to freedom of expression and the right to earn a decent living to the best of your ability. If being a prostitute is what you can do best, I don't see why it's illegal.

I can't fit prostitution into the Ten Commandments, but it goes in the Bible. Many prostitutes worked in Biblical times. Jesus told one of them, Ruth, that she should have no fears of hell. Jesus said, "It's not what you do physically, it's what's in your heart that counts." He assured Ruth that she'd go to heaven. I may too.

INDIVIDUAL ENTREPRENEURS

SOLANGE

INDIVIDUAL
ENTREPRENUERS

$\mathcal{SOLANGE}$
an Independent Call Girl

SOLANGE: I don't think there are any men. I don't think
there's one man left. I was married twice—to two babies. I
don't have sex with them any more, but I still baby them.
I forgive them for not taking care of me. I still call them
coochy, coochy. I baby my boyfriend, Don, like you wouldn't
believe. I've never asked for anything from either of my
husbands or my boyfriend. With my first husband, I felt he
owed me some help, but I didn't ask, because I thought,
because of his greediness, he would say no. I can't take
rejection, so I decided to ask for nothing. My second husband

didn't have any money to give to me.

Actually, I didn't want to take money from just anybody. I wanted to have my own achievement. That's why I started as a call girl. Now I take from men, but that's my accomplishment—they pay me for my work.

SOLANGE: I worked as a model while I was married to my second husband. The money was good, but I paid for the jobs—with my body. It took me some time to realize what I was doing. A photographer would call me to his studio and say he could get me work. Then he'd offer me a drink and seduce me. The more photographers I screwed, the more work I got. I was very busy.

Just after I left my second husband, my best friend, Sally, started working as a call girl. I was beginning to add the figures for myself. For every hour I modeled for fifty dollars, I had to fuck at least once. I was getting paid for fucking *and* modeling. I began to think that if I had to screw anyway I might as well limit myself to screwing and make the same money without the hassle of modeling.

I just couldn't believe my eyes when I saw Sally doing it for twenty-five dollars, When you've never been a prostitute. you feel that if you're going to sell yourself, the man should at the minimum buy you an old abandoned castle in Germany. Minimum.

Think of Madam Pompadour or Du Barry. Whoever made it in this occupation. Courtesans. Think of Louis the Somebody going to her, fucking her, and giving her one rose. And think of the same Louis giving her a palace as a present. The day she got the rose, she felt—it was romantic, but nothing. But when he gave her a very expensive present—he spent money and time to get that present. She felt valuable and wanted. But twenty-five dollars!

My family were aristocrats when Napoleon was emperor. Then they settled in Argentina and flourished as landed gentry until radical political regimes took away their property. If my mother were to ask me what I was doing now, I'd say: Well, you know, I have some good friends. My mother wouldn't think a thing of that. It's normal for a girl who has fallen from riches to have friends who help her maintain her style.

One duke who has no money now—he and his wife charge twenty-five thousand dollars to go to your party. Why is that not called prostitution? All I ask is a lousy hundred bucks and I'm called a whore. His Highness doesn't say: Hey man, you have to pay twenty-five grand. But someone in his entourage will say: His Highness has a pain in the ass. I'm sorry that he has to decline the invitation. That implies that His Highness is broke. So then you send him a check for twenty-five thousand and His Highness appears. He never mentions the fact that he received the check. He doesn't say thank you. I prefer to do business on these terms. The world owes it to me. I don't feel guilty or immoral. That I've fallen into financial disgrace is not my fault. Only people who belong to my social level understand this principal. They will come up with things for me.

People of the lower classes are idiots. That's why the men are called Johns. Those girls are called whores because they are stupid. If they were not stupid, they wouldn't be prostitutes. Actually, they're born to be prostitutes. There's nothing else they can do. Fuck and get *paid*. It's tit for tat and the end of that. I am an aristocrat with no occupation and no source of income, so this has become my way of life. In my position, this is the only way I can make the kind of money I deserve.

When I was married between the ages of eighteen and twenty-eight, I hadn't discovered myself as a woman. Or as a person. I was grateful to my husbands for keeping me. I had a small sense of myself and I was thankful for whatever I got. I didn't feel I deserved either love or material gifts. That's been the most radical change in my life. When I started to be paid, I felt that I was being given a present for being a beautiful lady. I began to analyze myself and my relationships.

Should any woman go out with a man just because he's nice looking? Meanwhile he's fucking the hell out of her and one day he drops her like a hot potato. And what does she get? Zero. Not a cent.

Maybe she had to take the Pill and meanwhile she's had abortions. He, he looks marvelous because he's gotten everything he wanted from her and good-bye!

Let's say a girl had a lot of friends and hadn't made up her mind about going steady with one of them. But Bill takes her to the mountains skiing. Wouldn't she feel like he cares a lot, because he took her on a trip? But what about if Bill takes all the other girls to the mountains and doesn't take her anyplace. He comes home and fucks her and leaves her. How does she feel? Like shit? True.

I've learned that the only way a man can show his appreciation is to give you presents. Period. It makes me feel a man is true. When I receive enough money, he shows he cares.

I make a man know, in a subtle way that I love jewelry or furniture or flowers. Whatever I love. I don't happen to love anything material. I've had money and it has no mystery for me. But now I need money, so I make men pay. If I were a wealthy girl at this moment, I wouldn't accept money. But don't think men wouldn't have to be very happy to invite me to London or Davos or the opening of a Broadway play. That costs them money too. A man must always show his interest in you with material things. Otherwise he's taking. And you are being taken.

The first year in the business, you're learning. The learning process is very long—like going to school. Handling men is a science. You have to know how to answer all the time. How to be in control. Before I entered the life, I never thought about controlling men. I just let them take me—in. Now I had to learn to look at a man and read his special needs. This came through time, experience, and serious study.

I met the very best men on the straight level. I'd go with a friend to have lunch or drinks at a very nice place—the Sherry Netherlands, the Drake. That's how I made big money—with men who I met out. Then the man meets me as a *woman*. I'd get his card, but never give out my number because "I'm going to Europe"—always some big lie. Then I'd call him a week later and invite him for cock-tails. He'd come over and I'd talk to him. "Oh, I like your tie." "Oh, you made such a good impression on me." That bullshit. He doesn't feel he's met a hooker. If he's married, he feels he's met someone he could have an affair with. If he's single, he's met a girlfriend.

The second time the man comes for cocktails, I'd take him to the bedroom and make him take off his clothes. I'd never get undressed myself. I don't know if he's a policeman. Alone or in company, a cop who feels he has to pay will always scare a girl. So with all this romance and kisses and embraces and the little petting of the cock, I take him to bed and kiss, kiss, kiss. "Oh, sweetheart, take your jacket off." "Oh, that tie is squeezing your beautiful neck." "Oh, take that belt off." I'd make him undress. The man would always try to make me undress too. But, "Oh, no. You get undressed and then I'll give you a beautiful striptease." So when he was undressed, I'd still be dressed. Then I'd say, "Sweetheart, do you have a hundred dollars for some flowers or some scotch?"

He'd say, "Gee, I didn't know I was going to have to pay."

"Oh darling, you don't pay. But today, let's pretend you brought me some flowers." So he'd say he didn't have a hundred, but he had fifty. So I'd get fifty. But if he said he wasn't counting on anything like this and doesn't have the money, then I'd keep kissing and kiss-ing until the phone rang and, "Oh, I have an appointment with my lawyer. You have to leave." I learned never to do a thing for nothing.

If the man did come up with the money, then I'd undress. Once a policeman is undressed, he cannot make an arrest. Meanwhile, if he's not a cop, I would have collected, which meant I was in control of time. I have to do just enough to get him out of the apartment.

Whatever a man gave me—if he gave me a hundred, or, if he was wearing a big diamond, I knew I could ask for two or three hun-dred, that will be his minimum for the future. He could never come to see me for less than that.

I was surprised to find that I could control men. I experimented with techniques. I'd give them a bubble bath with oil. I'd say, "I was going to take a bath, but I waited for you." Always FOR YOU. I'd never wet a finger. They'd think I was going to. I'd get them in the tub and massage them. "Please, that steam is good for you." "Try to cough and clear your system." I'd go through these lines of bullshit and enjoy it. I didn't feel like I was doing something wrong. I was proud of myself. I'd get them in bed and put baby powder all over them and shake it off. Then I'd give them a little blow job and they'd come in two seconds. I learned that it was all in the atmosphere. I never treated men badly. I'd treat them like regular children, and they loved it. I reminded them of their favorite nanny.

A girl in the street has to fuck. The difference between a call girl and a streetwalker is the gift of talk. I seldom actually fuck, because I learned to create an erotic atmosphere with language.

"I'll give you so much pleasure. I'll have an orgasm just watching you have fun. I'll do everything." But I didn't let them touch me. It was easy. I'd touch him on the nipples and ask, "Do you like that?"

He'd say, "Yes, I like everything. Let me do it to you now."

"You'll do it later." I'd never say, "You will do it to *me* later." I'd say, "Later, later, later." Or, "Slowly, don't touch me, because I'm too sensitive, too sexy. I'll tell you when I'm ready." Then when he was ready, he'd be coming because he thought I was ready too. Ready for me was when he came! But the men never know.

I'd kiss the nipples and give them little bites in the ribs. Occasionally, I'd have a fellow who was very voluminous, so I'd play with his navel and under his arms. I'd go bring hot towels and put them between his legs. This makes it easy for a fellow who has trouble getting a hard-on. I put hot towels on the testicles and the cock and ass. I'd make him really warm. And he'd think I was going to start doing it, but no, no, no. Then I'd bring the baby oil and another towel. I'd work the baby powder in with my hands. Notice I wasn't working with my pussy and no one was touching my boobs. I wasn't sucking anything. I was talking a lot of beautiful things a man wants to hear. "I love you." "You're so beautiful today." "You're the most beautiful man in the whole world."

He'll say," Please don't turn me off." He thinks I'm putting him on.

"But I'm telling you something I really feel at this moment. You're the type of man I desire today. Don't turn *me* off. You're going to make it sound like words. Please let me have fun." And I'd go on and on. By the time he was ready to be worked on, he already had an erection—tender like a little lamb, because no one does all this to him. Believe me, his wife doesn't—and neither do most lower-class call girls and hookers.

Men love it when a girl kisses their ass. Most girls tell me about the pigs who want to "go around the world." I can understand that this is not something everyone likes to do. But the more you do to a man, the faster he gets out of the bedroom. And the less he'll wear and tear you.

I clean them off very well, of course. And I make them ready by the time I get down there. Usually, I just put my face near, blow hot air and work with the knuckle of my hand. That feels like a tongue. Some men's asses are very ugly, but if they ask, "Nothing but my pleasure." I usually don't let them ask, because, if they have to ask, I feel put down. So I DO it. And no girl would unless she was asked to, so I get men crazy.

Then I turn them over and massage them. And oh, I have big tickling matches too. A fellow in his sixties—I tickle him all over and say, "You're my baby, you're my darling. Now I'm your mommy. No, now you're my daddy and I'm your baby." If he laughs, I start to play like a child with him. That makes a man feel like a very young child—for a while. He's so happy. And if he's happy, that's good business for me.

Occasionally a man will ask, "What do you have that's new?" So I put half an aspirin and pulverize it with a little sugar and feed him. I say it's some fantastic Oriental drug, and they get high on it. Their eyes dilate and they think they've had some exotic drug. One man asked, "Do you think I can leave? How long will this last?"

I've learned to do all this talk and make propaganda about how much fun we're going to have, but when they reach for the boobs or they want to kiss me with their tongue, why should I? It's not that I hate it. The name of the game is to make as much money as you can without work. Why should I let them wear and tear me? There is no work in the bedroom if you're good. The guy is laying there and you kiss and caress him, lick him, and suck him. And when you're through, you say, "Stay there and relax. Take a fast nap. I'm going to wash up and I'll bring you a nice warm towel. You can watch the news." I put the TV on. "How about another drink?" So he'll think I'm ever so solicitous. And I enjoy doing it that way. I really do. That way I don't feel guilty. I gave nothing of me.

These are your rules. This is your salesmanship. If you're going to sell clothes, you're given training in all the different philosophies for success in selling. You learn how to answer, how to close a deal. In this business, you're always closing a deal. And you have to have the answer ready for every question. All this takes self-examination and a study of men. I'd started on a new learning course when I became a call girl.

A girl should never get into the business unless she knows she's a good salesman. If a man tells me, "Oh, you have beautiful eyes," I might think my eyes look like shit, but I would never tell him, "Oh come on. Don't be silly. Do you mean it?" I say, "It's beautiful, darling." If he says it's beautiful, should I knock down my merchandise? If you don't like your merchandise, you can't sell it. You cannot sell fabric if you do now know how that fabric is made and you can't speak well of it. This is the same thing. You have to be very secure that you're the greatest. At conning!

As an independent call girl, you usually "reciprocate" with about fifteen other girls. We don't take cuts from each other for the dates we send. Instead, if I send a girl a Hundred,* she has to reciprocate— or send me another Hundred in return. If I just took a cut, I'd get forty dollars—one time. In reciprocation, I have a chance to cultivate that man—make him come back to *me* again and again. He'll also refer his friends. One reciprocation can turn into thousands of dollars. A cut is a measly forty. Period.

I would prefer to solicit all my men in elegant nightspots, start them as dates, romance them, and hit them for a pile. But this tech-

* *A date who regularly pays a hundred dollars.*

nique takes time and patience, and months pass when I need quick money, so I play for pass-arounds. Early in the game, I started meeting masochists—guys that wanted to be peed on—these fascinated me. I was disgusted and amused. I had my first one with Sally. He was wearing red bikini panties—the kind that open in the front for the pussy to show through. His cock was hanging out. He had on a girdle and garter belt with black stockings.

He came into the room and said to Sally, "I want to be your slave, mistress." So Sally ran to me and said, "Jesus Christ, this guy is crazy. I don't know what to do with him."

I said, "Just tell him, 'Son of a bitch, get on your knees!'"

She said, "How did you know? Did you ever do it?"

"No, but I saw it in the movies."

"Please come in with him."

I said, "No, tell him that he seems so stupid that you're going to call your girlfriend to watch. Then I appear. Otherwise I have no reason. But after that, I'll do your part."

She says to the guy, "You're so ugly, you're so fat and you look so stupid in women's clothes. Let me call my girlfriend to see you."

I came in and had a ball. He had one of the hugest cocks. Do you know that most masochists have a huge cock—the fellows that want to do it Greek and masochists have a big cock?

I said, "You son of a bitch."

He said, "This is my cock." Purring, he was.

"Don't touch it, pig. Listen, you motherfucking cock." I love dirty words. The first time I heard motherfucker on the street, I laughed. This was a beautiful way for me to use foul language.

He said, "I won't let you suck my penis, mistress."

I got vicious. "How dare you!" Let me see you play with your cock." Most girls are dumb. They go and suck the guy, and the man doesn't really want it, even though he asks. I instinctively knew how to treat a masochist. I loved it. I discovered the sadistic strain in me.

I began to do a lot of masochists. When I'm treating one, I really feel it. It freaks me out. I want to beat the hell out of them. I don't know what I'm doing, but God, do I enjoy myself. I'm just in heaven.

I have one guy who I put in the bathtub and stick two hairbrushes at one time in his ass. I put toothbrushes up—anything I can find in the bathroom. Then I pee on the guy. He has an erection and comes all over the place.

A girl might think that she's putting the guy down by degrading him, but, in the meantime, he's paying her, so that's his putdown already. A masochist will always try to pay less. That's a rule of the game. A masochist is a Fifty * and even if you work hard, you won't get an extra nickel from that Fifty. That is his putdown. His putdown on you. His guilt for letting you see him as his true self.

That's why, when I do a masochist, I really want to kill him. I don't want to stop at anything but murder. I can't stop myself. I go black. I can't see a thing. Everything's black. I get so desperate that, out of that desperation, I go blank.

Actually, I wish I didn't freak out, because I'd like to give every John a spanking. If that's what they want so badly, why not? I began to feel that the business was a circus—I was watching all these mentally retarded men. Like I was being given a special function for backward boys. To me, tricks are mentally unbalanced. That's why I baby them. At first, I couldn't believe these guys had ever graduated from anything—that they were lawyers and bankers. All tricks have something that makes them look like each other—wall eyes and blank—like mongoloids.

The pass-arounds that I'd get from girls by reciprocation—some woudn't even take their clothes off. They'd leave their pants and shirt and tie on. They don't know me and they're scared.

Sometimes men walked into the door and didn't want me. One fellow wanted a very feminine girl. When he saw me, he said no. I got insulted and went to the mirror: What's so hard-looking about me? Why does he not think I'm feminine when everyone else does?

So I gave him my friend Lilly's telephone number and said, "Please darling, she's a lovely girlfriend of mine—she's very, very feminine."

He said, "Is she *very* feminine?" I knew Lilly would satisfy him.

* *A date who regularly pays fifty dollars.*

"Yes, she's a little doll." By little doll, he thought I meant a short girl with big boobs. Lilly could understand that man's philosophy more than I, because she'd been hustling all her life.

He was disappointed when he saw her and she said, "I know just what you want. I have a girlfriend who has been gifted by nature."

He said, all excited, "Yah?" That's what he wanted.

I had one very funny character who wanted to race around the table taking our clothes off. He walked into the apartment, his eyes gleamed and he said, "Oh, you're tall!" I always make myself up nicely. He said, "You're tall and you're so pretty. And your eyes. Oh, you look like a ballet dancer." A ballet dancer this tall! He hadn't seen a ballet dancer in his life. Then he said, "You look like a showgirl."

"I am a showgirl." I am what he wants, right?

He said, "Oh, what long legs you have. I'm sure you can run fast."

"I'm sure I can beat you." That did it. I'm running around the table taking my clothes off and so is he. I'm running so fast he can't touch me. Finally, I take my robe and panties off and he jumps on them and yells "GERONIMO." And he comes on my panties.

I was shocked. He'd evidently not done this with anyone else. But I also couldn't hold my laughter. I'm still laughing. I did spend a few hours on my knees cleaning semen off the carpet.

I asked the girl I met him through: "What does he usually do?"

She said, "I didn't want to tell you, because you give the men a little more time with talk, but he always bothers me by asking what shows did I see or have I ever been to the horse races." I see now that the showgirls have long legs and so do horses, but she didn't make that connection. He must have made it with some track queen back home. I wonder what these men do with their wives?

Lilly called one day to say she had a fellow who needed a nurse—he doesn't want to feel it's business. Lilly had a lot of these mental games, which I hate. Lilly insisted I take him. "He wants an enema. He'll bring his own." She says, "He goes, takes a poop and that's all."

This man was supposed to be a Fifty, but Lilly told him that this nurse—me—was a Hundred. She owed me a hundred-dollar date and was trying hard to reciprocate. Lilly was a genius. What a woman! She could make any man spend more money. "This nurse is special." Incredible—the men would pay.

Well, this fellow comes here. I should have ordered an ambulance. He had a long rubber hose—almost a yard. I was flabbergasted, but all right. I looked at the hose and it still had feces on it—the thing hadn't been sterilized. I said, "Look, I wouldn't mind treating you, but this hose hasn't been sterilized."

He said, "Just boil it in a pot."

I said, "Pardon me. In my cooking pot? No." So I told him I had a syringe for douching. He wanted me to wear jockey pants—I put on his. I should give him an enema wearing men's underwear!

Then he goes to the bathroom and asks if I have any dirty literature. I had a beautiful collection of magazines. He's sitting there and I hear all these terrible noises—sounds like Vietnam. He relieved himself and that was that. Then he said, "Please call another nurse."

I sent him to Maria and then he called me back. I said, "Please call Lilly." So Lilly sent him to Rachel on the West Side. He must have had enemas from every girl in New York that day.

When he left, I had to go downstairs and buy Lysol and room spray and burn incense and bay leaves. For days I kept thinking the house stunk. Everytime I think about him I die. I don't see how I did it. But you learn.

You learn to take care of the fantasies. Once Lilly sent me a man without warning. He saw me and said, "Aren't you a cute little girl." I knew that message.

I said, "Yeah, you bastard. You like little girlies."

He says, "Yeah, they have no hair on their pussy." I sat on his lap and pretended to be a little girl, but it's really all in the talking. His pleasure is going to come when he hears that a featherless bird is sitting on his lap and suddenly his cock gets very hard when he hears it's pushing against the featherless pussy. I say, "She moves away with her short skirt lifted, and then you see her thighs from the back. And you will accidently touch her and she turns around and says, 'What's that thing between your legs, Uncle Jack.' " I keep talking, because it's a mental game. But no matter how good an imagination you have, it's never enough. These men are freaks and not very elegant.

Very few dates I got by reciprocation were elegant men. They paid fifty or a hundred, and I began to feel undervalued and underappreciated. The only men I didn't feel this way about were men that gave me plenty—men that showered me with gifts and money. They weren't Johns. They were gentlemen. They took pride in me as a lady. They'd love me and take me on special trips and buy me diamonds. But these men dried up with the recession. That kind of money wasn't to be had. So I had to put up with guys who came to use me and gave me peanuts.

I got to the point where I was very afraid of Johns. I didn't trust them. It was awful for me to meet someone for the first time, because I was conscious that they had come to my house to be laid. That therefore they were going to pay and degrade me. If I had to go out on a date, I couldn't get into the elevator by myself. I had to have the doorman ride up with me. I'd tremble and sweat. I knew this fear was sick, that it was associated with being paid for sex at the end of the ride. But as long as I'm in this business, elevators will terrify me if I don't know the man.

A girl in my circle might reciprocate a date and tell me he's an angel. But how do I know he's an angel? He might have been darling to her, but me—I might be just the kind of girl he always wanted to hurt.

I am not afraid because I've had bad experiences. I protect myself against them. I've never had any sort of trouble with the police. No clever girl does. I change my number often and check all my dates.

I've had a couple of experiences with a man getting a little offhand. In front of certain people, I get frightened. I don't know why. But then I develop a liver attack, and oh gee, I've got to go home.

The first year a girl gets in this business—if she's a loner like me—she buys furniture and mink coats, clothes and shoes. Ornaments for herself. All girls seem to have a thing about wallpaper in the bathroom. They want to paper their walls with money. These girls must have had an outhouse when they were growing up and wiped themselves with newspapers. Suddenly they have a bathroom! There's some luxury about that room for them. I like a beautiful bathroom too. But I don't have to glue dollars on the wall to make it nice.

I learned to keep very accurate records. I recorded every man I saw in a day book. In case someone would find it, I'd write, Tuesday, 2:00, Mr. and *Mrs.* Jones. Money I always wrote in small figures. "The week closed at fifteen." That means fifteen hundred. Records are kept because this is a business like any other business. If you know you made two thousand last week, and now you don't have a cent, where did it go? I paid the electric bill, the telephone bill, the rent, and Bergdorf.

I compare from one year to the next. If I made two thousand in the first week of March last year, then I should make more in that week this year. It's business and you want to improve.

The minimum any girl should make is two hundred dollars a day. If you can't make that, you should get out of the business. Once you're in the business, you have big expenses. Liquor. And you always have to have something cute in the refrigerator. A beautiful spinach salad. The date says, "I'm on my lunch hour." "Have you eaten, darling?" "Well, I don't have much time." "Come on, I have something special for you." You make him a cute little canape that makes him feel he got more from you and that you really care for him. I always plan that way, but it costs money.

Then clothes and lingerie cost money. I have fellows who like to wear girls' clothes, which they inevitably rip apart. I can't just have one outfit, because three or four "dressers" might show up on one day. Dick's only thirty and he comes up here and puts on a skirt and panties and just jerks himself off while he says, "I'm a whore, I'm a son-of-a-bitch whore." He calls me by some male name and says, "Gee, I wish I could work too. If I had a pussy, I'd be making a fortune." Cheap Johns are all whores at heart. That's why I can't have any feeling for them.

A rare date I'll have some feeling for and that costs me too. Pete had cancer in his pancreas. He was going to die last summer and I spoiled him rotten. I figured, poor man, he's going to die, so let him die happy. I gave him so much sex like he's never had before in his life. Every time I saw him, I couldn't see a soul afterwards, because he took such a long time to come. But I enjoyed it, because for once I was doing something good. And he adored me. I felt he should die happy. With one good fuck.

I'd pass him around—give him other girls' numbers. I wanted him to go, but no—he wanted me. He didn't die, but now he always calls me and says he's broke. If I go to dinner with him, he might spend three or four hundred dollars—food, theater, tipping everybody just to show off—not to show off to anyone, but to show himself to me. He doesn't want to pay any more. He's "my friend." I can't afford friends unfortunately. They create problems. They make demands on my time and don't produce cash.

One evening when business is slow, a friend of Solange's, who is in her circle of call girls, drops by for a visit.

ROXANNE: *Hey, I want something to eat.*

SOLANGE: *A salad?*

ROXANNE: *Don't you invite me over when you're having steak for dinner? What do you think I am? A rabbit?*

SOLANGE: *You don't understand. This man living with me eats like a Hungarian refugee. So I just buy enough food to get by. To try to give him the hint. He's not co-operating with the groceries. And I found I was paying two hundred dollars a week to feed him.*

ROXANNE: *Why don't you tell him, man? You want fifty dollars a week for the grocery bills. Every week. And you buy the groceries with that money and that's it. Why should he pay for the groceries when you're so good-hearted?*

SOLANGE: *I have enough groceries for me. But I'm just getting what I need. Another thing you know. When you're*

SOLANGE: *in this work, you can't have any groceries. All it takes is one visit and the John thinks he has refrigerator privileges.*

[Solange sets a place for Roxanne and makes a flourishing presentation of the salad.]

ROXANNE: *Hey, this is very good. You're a fabulous cook.*

SOLANGE: *I don't cook so much, 'cause I work. I don't sit around in bed like you and then cook for myself all the time.*

ROXANNE: *You trying to tell me something? Men don't call me anymore. They don't want to fuck me anymore. And my girlfriends don't call me, 'cause they're afraid I'm going to take their men away.*

SOLANGE: *That's not what it's all about. I know, because it's happening to me. You hate the business. You don't know what the fuck to do for a living and you know you have to do something. So you sit in bed when you wake up and you watch TV and you don't call one John.*

ROXANNE: *I did. All the months I was up in that apartment.*

SOLANGE: *Somehow you pay the rent. And you bought a new coat and a new TV.*

ROXANNE: *Yeah.*

SOLANGE: *When you call, it works. When you go out, guys turn around and look at you. They all want you. If you don't want to fuck them, you give them your number. Get the guy to come for a drink. He's having a great drink, and meanwhile you tell me he's coming. So I call you fifty times and he thinks that people do call you. He's going to want to meet somebody and you say a hundred. See what I mean? Now the girls —like Sally—they think you don't give them any men, so they don't give you anything.*

ROXANNE: *But that's not true.*

SOLANGE: *I know it's not true, but they think . . .*

ROXANNE: *It's just not the truth. I gave Sally hundreds and she gave me nothing.*

SOLANGE: *You know what the problem is? When they give you something, they know they're giving you one of their steady guys, and you give them a man you just got by chance. If you didn't say anything to the girl— even me, your friend—just here's a date, then she's a worker. You shouldn't tell any of us anything.*

ROXANNE: *I'm sure one of the reasons girls don't give me their business is that I'm much too old now. Over forty I am. The market is for girls in their early twenties. On the telephone. The regular Johns don't want me.*

SOLANGE: *You're wrong. Any business—whether it's restauranteurs, whoring, the clothes business, or art galleries —it's personality and knowledge. And neither has a thing to do with age.*

ROXANNE: *I have several girlfriends who think that most of the business is for young girls.*

SOLANGE: *Just get them to come. If they complain, you say, "Sweetheart, next time let me introduce you to someone to be unfaithful to me with. I have divine girlfriends."*

ROXANNE: *That's another reason girls don't give me their good dates. They know I'm going to grab them and madam them. And I do do it. I pay for the privilege of doing anything I can with the guy. I pay by giving the girl dates of mine. She has the same chance. The trouble is they all come back to me.*

SOLANGE: *Well, let's say a guy comes to you and you can see he doesn't want you. You immediately say, "Sweetheart, shall we call a divine girl. I have a friend who just arrived from Italy." Whatever you think he wants. "A Russian girl." Well, he doesn't like Russian girls. But you have a French girl and here I come, Parlez-vous. Or whatever.*

ROXANNE: *I don't have a problem in that area. It's age.*

SOLANGE: *Men are for young girls for one reason only. They can really hustle them. They go for a young girl because she lets him do anything he wants.*

ROXANNE: *I don't believe that. Why do I want to fuck young men? Because I don't like fucking old men. Well, for the same reason, these guys want a young girl. If they want to fuck old women, they can fuck their wives. A lot of men just want to fuck pretty young girls. The young girl is softer and not so hard. Whereas, the old girl is tough and smart—she can get him off in two seconds. Whereas me, I took Robert home, got him into bed and had him off in a half a minute. He didn't want to get off, but he got off like that. I've made a career out of sucking a guy off before he can get into me. I'm so good at it, because I hate to fuck. I hate to have Johns come in me in the worst way. Men want a young girl, because they can pull out on her and stop. I'm going to get him, boom.*

SOLANGE: *With these young girls, they get tired of fucking and stop and meanwhile he has her eating his ass and his balls. I tell you the truth, if I have a young girl working for me, I have to stay away from it, because she doesn't listen. I tell her to suck, and she says, I hate sucking cock. But if I suck, I keep my years and my youth longer. If you fuck, you lose your youth.*

ROXANNE: *I send a young girl out on a date and she comes back two hours later and I ask her what the fuck were you doing for two hours. "Well, he wanted to talk." Fucking smoke is coming out of my ears.*

SOLANGE: *With all this business, why don't you work?*

ROXANNE: *Because I hate that fucking phone. I hate feeling that I have to call. My head's all messed up. I'm just getting back together again. I felt better when I had*

ROXANNE: *Lewis calling me up and getting me to have dinner with people. I don't like the aggressive telephone shit. I want someone to help me. Lewis didn't even take a cut—oh yes, a small piece of me. But so what. He set me up.*

SOLANGE: *I'd rather have dinner dates too. When I started in the business, I was having dinner dates almost every fucking night. But that business is finished.*

ROXANNE: *I want to be a society whore again. Romancing. Playing it like you really like the guy. "Darling, I haven't paid the rent." Or "Let's go to Cartier's." Play the romance. You know this guy has money, so you move in on him. He knows that he has to lay a few hundred on you for nothing. He knows he isn't going to get laid unless he comes across with that "loan." I love that game. I'd never come out and say, "You want to fuck me, it's a hundred or a thousand dollars." I'd meander around—"You know, I'd love to go out with you." When I started as a society broad, it was a career. I'd be up at 10 A.M. in the beauty shop, meet someone for lunch—I'd go out for lunch every day. If the guy that took me out wasn't going to give me money, I could meet ten guys in a fancy restaurant that would be good money. Fifteen years ago, money was flowing. I was up to my ass in men. Then I was young and I wasn't hip to what was going on. I was too dumb to make the really big scores. Now that I really know what to do—if I only looked like I did when I was twenty-five! It was a freshness and naïveté that I can't recapture. I very quickly learned which guys would give you money, and which guys would just take you out and fuck you. If you just wanted to go out to El Morocco, you still could make connections. You may have to fuck this guy and he may not give you money that night,*

ROXANNE: *but you may meet seven guys that you can really score big from.*

SOLANGE: *I remember sitting at a table, seeing a guy, and locking eyeballs. Then I'd go for a walk to the ladies' room and get the guy to give me his card. Then I'd meet him. That was great.*

ROXANNE: *When I did do it, I eventually managed to grab one of those men off and get them to keep me. And then I'd stop it. I couldn't wait to stop, because I hate it. But I'm lazy and there's no eaiser way to make this kind of money. For me. There's nothing else that I'm qualified to do that isn't a lot of hard work. I do not like work. I don't like dealing with people in business. I have no success drive whatsoever. My idea of a complete life is having someone to fuck, having food in the refrigerator, and a couple of friends. Enough money to go traveling around and having a good time. I'm not interested in being a star. I'm not interested in being a businesswoman. I just want to fuck and enjoy life. I want to do it with as little effort as possible.*

SOLANGE: *Don't you think everyone feels the same way?*

ROXANNE: *Well, at least this way, we boss ourselves. I call the shots. I used to take my Johns and turn them into lovers. Now I'm taking my lovers and turning them into Johns.*

SOLANGE: *You can't fall in love with a John. You wonder why I don't fall in love with a man who takes me shopping and spends a lot of money. It's a disease. Whoring is a mental disease. And the men that pay are whores too. They just can't get anyone to pay them.*

ROXANNE: *I resent having them pay me to fuck them. Although I'm taking the money, I don't like it. I resent having to fuck to get money, but meanwhile I will fuck them because I need that money badly. I love fuck-*

ROXANNE: *ing. But not with Johns. I value fucking and that's why it's so hard with the John. I place value on myself. I think I'm somebody—not just a whore. But I need money, and fucking's the easiest way to get it.*

SOLANGE: *Well, we've studied the program. The only whores who do, went down all the way, and from real suffering went up. I think we're in that process now.*

ROXANNE: *I've almost crippled myself. I don't want to do anything, so I don't do anything. If I put myself out, I can make money, like that. But there are certain things I have a total block against. But when I got into the swing with Lewis and he was calling me up, I moved very well. But I can't fuck anymore unless it's a quick, easy Hundred. I'd rather someone else did it. I could have had madam's businesses—but I don't want anything big. That only means trouble. And you have to deal with all kinds of men. I don't like that. For a whore, I'm a big snob. I'm very touchy about my people and who I deal with. I walked into the Regency one day, and there were twenty-five men in the room. I walked out. No, I ran. I cannot deal with that situation. I have to have the embroidery. I have to have the fantasy. I cannot deal with the crude.*

SOLANGE: *I have to have it dressed up too. But I can do it the other way.*

ROXANNE: *Not me. It has to be good taste. If I'm a whore and I'm there for money, I still don't want to be treated as a whore. I don't want to be in an atmosphere where I'll be put down. In bed, I can be the filthiest mouth, most perverted freak in the world—if that's what he's looking for. In the bed. But before I get into that bed, no. I want discretion.*

SOLANGE: *You don't understand the reason you have contempt for the John. I know. In the back of my mind, I now*

SOLANGE: *know that the man who pays for sex is sick and that I make my living off the sickness of that man. The whole world calls us nasty because we make men pay. But we're just satisfying their sickness.*

ROXANNE: *That's why I use all men now. Even the pretty ones. I make them spend money. I've never met a man that could support me that I liked. They're all Johns. Doctors, lawyers, they bore me. I've been out with the most exciting men today. I cannot relate to some fucking lawyer. They bore me to fucking tears. I like corrupt men. Because I'm corrupt. But for Johns, give me a night romancing one guy. I don't want to fuck five guys for fifty.*

SOLANGE: *I'd rather fuck them for fifty. Then get a thousand from a guy by talking. The con game is a challenge that insults me. To me, hustling is too much work. I have to use the good side of my brain for money? It bothers me.*

ROXANNE: *You're not greedy enough.*

SOLANGE: *I am greedy.*

ROXANNE: *Then you don't work hard enough.*

SOLANGE: *I don't feel like working.*

ROXANNE: *What do you think? They're going to come after you?*

SOLANGE: *I make money, don't I?*

ROXANNE: *Yes, but you shouldn't begrudge yourself the good money and conning. The only difference between you and the girl in the street is the con—your mind. You're not selling anything different. Yours isn't gold-lined.*

SOLANGE: *But the pimp thinks for the street girl. I have to use my own brain and it bothers me to use it for that purpose. I'm like pimping myself.*

ROXANNE: *I divorce myself from it.*

SOLANGE: *On my back, it's okay. But why should I use my*

SOLANGE: *genius on this. I hate to do it like hell.*

ROXANNE: *I cannot go into a bar and meet a man and turn around five minutes later and say, "Do you want to fuck me for fifty dollars?" I cannot. I cannot do it. Yet I can go to a fancy restaurant like the Regency and see a man cruising me and get his phone number and give him mine. Or have him take me to dinner and give him con and end up with money or not. To ask direct, I can't do it. And yet, if a friend calls and asks me to see a friend for a hundred and I get the whole rundown on him, beautiful. I can do it. I cannot go out there. It gives me the chills to think of it.*

SOLANGE: *I can speak to a guy nicely, but I don't want to mortify my brain. They're sick and they have to pay. They can see a psychiatrist or me. If they touch me, they pay. When you become a prostitute, that's where the sick is. But if you analyze it, you can make a business out of it.*

ROXANNE: *The girls just don't help anymore.*

SOLANGE: *The women in this business are awful now. If I call a girl who's supposed to be my friend and say I need a hundred dollars, she starts screaming "A hundred dollars. Why don't you go out and work?" And she hangs up the phone.*

ROXANNE: *Women used to be different. We used to take each other for dinner and we'd appreciate each other. Years ago, if I met a guy who had money and I could see he wasn't digging me, I'd make every effort to get him to one of my friends. A girl doesn't do this today. They've got their fucking pimps and gigolos. They've gotten very selfish. They don't appreciate each other.*

SOLANGE: *With women's liberation and the Pill, a girl can walk into a bar and decide she likes a guy and go*

SOLANGE: *home and fuck him. Girls wear themselves out. And they still know that what they want is to get married and none of the fucks she's getting is talking babies and marriage.*

ROXANNE: *There's a whole breakdown in values in life. Everyone's out to fuck everyone else before they fuck them. Friendship and honor and loyalty and manhood—they're all gone. There was never a time in my life when I was in a bar and got molested by a man when the bartender or some man around me wouldn't jump to protect me. Today the fucking bartender walks away when I get in trouble. I have to protect myself. Ten years ago that would never happen.*

No one can be your friend, because whoring right now is a very competitive business. You're being fucked from right to left—the massage parlors, streetwalkers, and nigger whores are all cutting up. Today, they don't put you down for being a whore. The only thing they can put you down for today is not making money. You can be a child murderer and it's all right as long as you're making money. That's the difference. When I started, there weren't that many whores around and we were condemned. I never gave a fuck about what people said, but they did talk. We girls stuck together like a sisterhood.

SOLANGE: *Now everyone's cutting everyone's throat. I think the whole business may be going out of style.*

ROXANNE: *There will always be a need for the business, but the prices are going down, because there're too many girls. The supply is far exceeding the demand!*

SOLANGE: *For a girl with a good head* [laughs] *, there'll always be money from the traveling businessman, the kooky freak, and, I hope, some rich handsome man who gets an idea that he wants a good time.*

SOLANGE: Girls I work with cause money problems. Now these girls are desperate to be in the business. They want money, but they think that by acting like a straight girl, they are going to land a fat date. My men who are Fifties and Hundreds are never going to be fat dates. Even if they are multimillionaires, they're just not going to part with their money. Fifty or a hundred is all you'll ever get. They're not looking for a lover among the prostitutes. If they want a lover, they meet a girl socially—not by reciprocation through me. My throat hurts explaining to these girls and they just don't understand. June does the same thing over and over. Now it's Angus Crocker. She says, "I'm stringing him along, because I'm going to get a pile." Meanwhile she fucks him twenty-five times and gets five hundred dollars. That's a twenty-dollar trick. Big deal. She turned a hundred-dollar date into a Twenty. That's stupid.

It's also putting me down. I introduce her as a call girl and she fucks for nothing. Like she's better than me. I am a true friend to girls. I've taken off my pantyhose for a girl. My clothes—I hardly have any. A girl comes and says something is pretty. I say, take it. Then she comes here and tells a guy I'm a whore and she's straight. She's supposed to reciprocate because I'm not taking a cut, and she never gives me one goddamn date. Not one date I get back from that girl. And she goes around saying I'm full of shit. That's the way she was brought up. To eat off her friends.

A girl like June—she makes men real whoremasters. Men call me and say, "Have you got anything new?" My men would never dare ask me that. They'd say, "Hello, sweetheart." And I'd say, "I think you're ready to meet a lovely girlfriend of mine." I'm the one that suggests they should go and meet someone new. I build the girl up—make her very cultured like me. I can always brush up her background. Like she could be a princess and I tell the guy she's a Russian princess. If I make her a little better, they'll respect her. They won't touch her. They just lay sprawled on the bed. That's my type. I don't want the wear and tear on me.

But these freebie girls are really stupid. June screws about two hundred guys a month and what does she get? The rent. I introduced her to a fellow here and she was for two and a half hours in the bedroom. I had to go open the door. What's she doing? Sitting in bed telling him the story of her life. They never even screwed. And the guy's sitting on the bed holding his head up to keep from falling asleep.

I have never been revengeful. But her. I am going to pull her hair one day. I mean it. She's taken so much advantage of me. She's borrowed cash, clothes, she eats here. A Pakistani refugee eats nothing compared to this girl. She's like a locust.

June takes pills—ups and downs and sideways. Everything. All the girls that go into the business are suicidal. There's a lack of self-esteem. The lack of fulfillment and achievement. Getting into the business is the last move before killing themselves. They feel: I failed in love, my career isn't doing the right thing for me, men haven't done the right thing by me, so goddamn, I'm going to charge them. They're all bitter against men. I'm just bitter about the fact that I have to charge them, because I like men.

I've planned to save money and get out. I'm not a compulsive prostitute. I can stop. Sure, I enjoy the masochists, but I'll find them somewhere else! I'm not a masochist myself.

My friend Lilly could never stop. Lilly loved fucking. In her own personal life, she never had the men she wanted. The business gave them to her—wealthy men, good-looking guys, fat, ugly degenerates that fulfilled her fantasies. She got the men she liked, number one.

Secondly, she worked to get money. The only way you can make big money in this business, is when you're tired you take an "up." And you don't say no to any calls. Lilly would take a sleeping pill and go to sleep. A half an hour later, the phone would ring and she'd get up and take an "up" and go and do the date. So she went from "down" to "up" to "down" to "up." She was such a calm girl that I never knew she was doing pills. I saw her take a couple, but she always made me believe that this was the first time in weeks. Her doctor told me she'd been taking pills for ten years.

Lilly was constantly discussing new angles to get money out of men. It was a big con game. I come right out with answers—but they're not as good as hers. She studied and thought. She would meditate for hours every day: How, if a man would say, "Let me light your cigarette," for example, she would say, "Oh, light me, please." She was constantly writing scripts in her mind.

Lilly would never let a man talk about anything but sex. I said, "Lilly, don't you get dizzy from talking about sex all the time. Can't you show the man a magazine or ask whether it's hot or cold out-side. Or where did he go last week. Or, "I haven't seen you in a month." "Oh no," she said. "When they're ready to leave, you might ask those questions. Otherwise, talk about sex." And she might have been right, because she always had repeats—men came back again and again.

Everybody was a real fuck for Lilly. She did everything. I might screw my guys, but I never fuck. On top, you can just move around on the tip of the cock, and when you feel they're ready to come, you fall forward. That way you don't punch your cervix.

Lilly looked worn out. She looked like a tired hooker. I tried to defend her to the other girls, but they'd say, "Come off it. Lilly looks like a cheap whore." But Lilly was the most expensive of them all. All the pass-arounds that were going for fifty, Lilly had them for a hundred—minimum. I'd send Lilly a Fifty, and I'd say, "This pass-around is a half." * She'd say, "Guess how much I got out of him? A hundred." Lilly was beautiful to work with. If I owed her a Fifty, I'd send her one, and she'd make him a Hundred from then on. Whoever she sent him to next, she'd say, "This gentleman is a cham-pagne." ** She was great.

Other than her techniques in business, I have no reason to admire her, because she was screwed up—oh, God. She'd fall in love with the wrong guy and suffer for him. The father of her son left her when she was eight months' pregnant. Always these weird love affairs. She fell in love with a real bastard John. The doctors thought he was going to die of cancer and Lilly visited him every day in the hospital. When he realized he didn't have cancer, he started to mis-treat Lilly: "You're a whore. I'm not going to marry you." That

* *Pays fifty dollars.*
** *Pays a hundred dollars.*

poor girl was trying so hard to get out of the business, just to please that damn trick.

I'd tell her she was masochistic, and she'd open her big black eyes. I'd say, "Yes, you are, you're masochistic." The way she did sex with men proved her masochism; the fact that she picked on the wrong guys proved her self-destructiveness. I told her these things. When Lilly was depressed, I'd tuck her into the sofa and cuddle her a little, bring her a pillow, and touch her hair. Then I'd give her milk to go to sleep. Sometimes I'd get so emotional doing this, I'd get tears in my eyes. I was not in love with the girl. I would never have thought of having sex with her. In this business, I'd learned to analyze myself and other people. Some people could go through the same emotions as me and think they're lesbians. They're not. I catch myself in time, because I know where it comes from—loneliness and a need for warmth. I don't confuse friendship with lesbianism.

When I met Lilly, I said, "One of these days, you're going to break my heart." I saw it. And she did. She killed herself. So many times I took a taxi to Lilly, because I knew she was going to be dead. Everyone said, "You're crazy." But she killed herself. I wasn't wrong. I felt so guilty. Like I didn't do enough for Lilly. I have moments of real sadness and loneliness, because Lilly was the one friend I had. We could talk about anything. I could trust her.

After Lilly died, I changed my phone number, because I got fed up with the Johns calling and saying, "It's my fault." Lilly and I used to think of our dates as friends, but after this, I call them all Johns. I don't think of them as dates even. Johns. No emotional involvement. Her particular John said, "I did love her. It's all my fault. She haunts me at night. I think I see her." This guy is an alcoholic, so he probably does hallucinate. "I can't leave my door unlocked, because I know Lilly's coming." He'd call me at three and four in the morning.

I was going to have Lilly's ashes at my house until I had prepared for the burial. Then a John I trusted called and I told him Lilly was dead and I was going to have the ashes. He said, "Can I come and jerk off on them?" He wanted to come on the ashes of the girl! Some guys are so crooked. I thought this guy was such a nice, straight date. But all men have a fantasy of some sort. I had to call Lilly's mother and tell her I couldn't have the ashes here. I found all Johns guilty. I was very impressed by Lilly's death.

I was lucky to be living with my boyfriend, Don, when Lilly died. I could have gone mad myself, but I had a man around. I have to have someone to love. Don gives me love in my life. I don't hate men.

Unfortunately, Don is broke. He came to me with one pair of pants and shoes that were falling apart. He's trying to be an actor and occasionally works as a bartender. I support him, but I forget about the fact that he doesn't have money. He has ambition, and to me that's worth more than money. If he had money, it would be very boring, because I have too many men like that. With Don—we are both working very hard to make it. He's the only man I've ever met that really wants to do something for me. He doesn't say so, but I know it. If he worked for himself alone, he couldn't. In a way, I've made a man out of him—he wants to do something for someone outside himself.

Don thinks I've gone to bed with seven guys in my life. He pushed me into confessing, so I started to talk like a hundred. He said, "Oh my God, you're a whore." I kidded. "No, ninety-nine." He was really angry. So I said, "About fifty." "About twenty-five." I kept looking at his face. I ended up at seven and that he put up with.

I had to make up all these lies. I'd say, "I'm thinking about going into the business. What do you think about it, darling?" Oh well, no, he wouldn't put up with this—not if I had to go to bed with anyone. Then I got the idea of being a madam. He got very suspicious. He'd say, "I don't believe you." I'd say, "Well, look, if all this fellow wants to do is jerk off, why should I pay a girl fifty or sixty dollars, when I can do it standing in the bathroom and get the whole hundred?" This sort of character I would confess I did. I didn't talk about the others. Actually, that was a lie, but it wasn't really a lie. I do the men, but I don't let them do me. Oh, some men like to kiss pussy. Occasionally I enjoy it. When my boyfriend did it to me a few times, it took me forever to get in ecstasies. Then, when

I'd be ready, I wouldn't come, because I'd feel guilty that I was putting him down. When the Johns did it, I loved it. I had this fantasy that it was a dog—that I was tied against a tree and a dog was sucking my pussy. In real life, I wouldn't let a dog get near me. But with the Johns, I think of dogs.

When I have sex with Don, I like to pull the blankets all the way up to my neck, turn the lights out, and have him seduce me. I'd say, no, no, no. I'd be very feminine and give him a chance to be the charger. A man. The hunter of the jungle.

But Don will never learn. He's not aggressive sexually. When we first met, we'd make love five, six, seven times in an evening and then we'd wake up and do it again. But every time he wanted it, he'd say, "Let's fuck." And I hate that. That language is for Johns, because they like it. But my lover—I don't take that sort of talk.

Don suddenly got suspicious of everyone. He drove me crazy with his jealousy. Between that and Lilly killing herself, I've lost my ambition. I want someone to come along and put me back where I belong. I've begun to feel that the business is a hustle. You have to constantly con people. Why should I make it for fifty when a guy opens his wallet and has three-thousand-dollars in there. Then I have to think fast of getting more out of him. Like I say, "Before it was for you, now let's do it for me." But that means I have to go to bed and work. And what does he give me? Another fifty.

Of course, I have new lines I can give him. "Let me think I'm the most beautiful thing that's happened to you in the last week. Please. Please, let me have a hundred." This talk I do, but I feel so put down talking this way. Girls in the street may be getting seventy-five from a John, but they are hard—they talk hard and enjoy being hard. I don't. I don't enjoy being cunning at all.

But all women are brought up to take goodies and then to give themselves in return. When Daddy comes home, he puts his hands behind his back and says, "Daddy's little girl want some candy?" Of course she does. "Well then, give Daddy a big kiss." She gives Daddy a kiss and gets the candy. We are *made* to be whores. The confusion comes as we grow older. We're told only to have sex with a man we love. So, if all the little girls are angels, men have to find women to pay for sex—women who they think are degraded and degenerate. Men create the need and then put down the women who fulfill it.

I don't feel degraded; I don't think I'm a freak. I just feel guilty when I don't get enough money. Then I feel I'm being paid and put-down. But I do want nice guys who spend money on me.

In one sense, this business has been therapeutic. I've regained my sense of self-esteem. I know I can earn my own way. It might be a silly or a dirty or a stupid way. But it's a way.